working with difficult & resistant staff

JOHN F. ELLER & SHEILA A. ELLER

Solution Tree | Press

a division of

Solution Tree

555 North Morton Street
Bloomington, IN 47404
800.733.6786 (toll free) / 812.336.7700
FAX: 812.336.7790

email: info@solution-tree.com
solution-tree.com

Visit **go.solution-tree.com/leadership** to download reproducible versions of selected figures in this book.

Printed in the United States of America

Library of Congress Cataloging-in-Publication Data

Eller, John Frank, III, 1957- , author.
  Working with difficult and resistant staff / John F. Eller, Sheila A. Eller.
      p. cm
    ISBN 978-1-935542-07-0 (perfect bound) -- ISBN 978-1-935542-08-7 (library edition)
1. School personnel management. 2. Problem employees. 3. School improvement programs. I. Eller, Sheila A., author. II. Title.
  LB2831.5.E395 2011
  371.2'01--dc22
                                    2010045881

Solution Tree
Jeffrey C. Jones, CEO & President

Solution Tree Press
President: Douglas M. Rife
Publisher: Robert D. Clouse
Vice President of Production: Gretchen Knapp
Managing Production Editor: Caroline Wise
Senior Production Editor: Risë Koben
Proofreader: Elisabeth Abrams
Text Designer: Orlando Angel
Compositor: Amy Shock
Cover Designer: Jenn Taylor

Acknowledgments

Solution Tree Press would like to thank the following reviewers:

Sonja Alexander
Director of Professional Learning
DeKalb County Schools
Decatur, Georgia

Nikki Cannon
Principal
Harbour Pointe Middle School
Mukilteo, Washington

Judith Martin-Tafoya
Principal
Truman Middle School
Albuquerque, New Mexico

Jacqueline Newton
Principal
Iroquois Ridge High School
Oakville, Ontario

Matilda Orozco
Principal
Lantrip Elementary School
Houston, Texas

Visit **go.solution-tree.com/leadership** to download reproducible versions of selected figures in this book.

Table of Contents

dA About the Authors

John F. Eller has had a variety of experiences working with adults over the years he has been in education. He has served in a leadership role for a new doctoral program at St. Cloud State University and worked with educational leaders at Virginia Tech University. He has held positions as director of Minnesota ASCD; director of a principal's training center; assistant superintendent for curriculum, learning, and staff development; and principal in a variety of settings. In addition to training and supporting facilitators, John specializes in dealing with difficult people; building professional learning communities; employee evaluation; conferencing skills; coaching skills; strategic planning strategies; school improvement planning and implementation; differentiated instruction; leadership for differentiation; employee recruitment, selection, and induction; supervisory skills; and effective teaching strategies.

John has a PhD in Educational Leadership and Policy Studies from Loyola University Chicago and an MS in Educational Leadership from the University of Nebraska at Omaha. He is the author of *Effective Group Facilitation in Education: How to Energize Meetings and Manage Difficult Groups* and coauthor of *So Now You're the Superintendent! Creative Strategies to Transform School Culture, Working With and Evaluating Difficult School Employees,* and the best-selling *Energizing Staff Meetings.*

Sheila A. Eller has worked in a multitude of educational settings during her career. She is currently an elementary school principal in the Mounds View Public Schools in Minnesota and has served as a principal in the Fairfax County Public Schools and in other schools in Minnesota and Illinois, a university professor, a special education teacher, a Title I math teacher, and a self-contained classroom teacher in grades 1–4.

In addition to her work in schools, Sheila has served education on a regional and national basis. She has been a member of the executive board of Minnesota ASCD and has been a regional president of the Minnesota Association of Elementary School Principals. She has completed advanced coursework in educational administration and supervision at St. Cloud State University and holds a master's degree from Creighton University, and a bachelor's degree from Iowa State University.

Sheila is a regular presenter at the ASCD national conventions, sharing her expertise on the topic of effective staff meetings and multiage instruction. While she worked at National-Louis University in Evanston, Illinois, she helped develop a classroom mathematics series that was adopted by several districts in the region. A video that accompanied this series featured her instructional techniques. In her work with educators, she specializes in energized staff meetings, school improvement initiatives, multiage teaching strategies, employee supervision, and teaching and learning in the content areas. Sheila is coauthor of the best-selling *Energizing Staff Meetings* and of *Creative Strategies to Transform School Culture* and *Working With and Evaluating Difficult School Employees*.

Preface
ɘɿ**ꟼ**

When we first started leading schools, change was somewhat optional. In today's high-stakes/high-accountability environment, school improvement and change are no longer optional. In past educational environments, we sometimes had the luxury of ignoring people who were resistant to change. Many leaders thought, "If we just give people more time, they will come along when they are ready." This attitude kept conflict to a minimum but also stalled many good change efforts. With increased school accountability, we can no longer ignore the behaviors of difficult or resistant people in our schools.

Many principals have told us that difficult or resistant people take up untold amounts of their time—both directly, in that they require supervision, and indirectly, in that principals must counter their influence on other employees in the school. The amount of energy principals put out trying to effectively manage difficult or resistant employees has not been tracked but would be mind-boggling if we could find a way to assess it.

Over the years, we ourselves have had the pleasure of working with many difficult and resistant people as we have led schools through improvement and change efforts. Many of these people have given us not only headaches and sleepless nights but also opportunities to learn and apply effective strategies to minimize their difficult and resistant behaviors. Even though we have not won every battle, we have been able to address their difficult behaviors head-on and actually turn some of them around. In all cases, by addressing the behaviors of difficult and resistant people, we have sent a message to the rest of our staff members that a few people cannot keep the rest of the group from moving forward.

As we have worked with other leaders over the years, we have found considerable apprehension and fear when it comes to attacking the behaviors of difficult and resistant people. We decided to put together our combined experiences and strategies and develop this book to help others who are facing people who cause trouble in their particular buildings. As we mentioned earlier, many of these difficult and resistant behaviors are a result of the efforts of school leaders to move their schools forward in the school improvement/change process.

This book has been designed with the practicing school leader in mind. The chapters are arranged in an order that makes sense for people first learning the skills of managing difficult and resistant staff members in a building. Even though there is a logical progression to the book, it has also been written so that busy practitioners can find information about their most pressing issues. Each chapter is designed to complement the rest of the material in the book but can stand alone as a resource. The chapters are brief enough to be read and digested quickly but contain enough focused information to help principals learn the strategies they need to make an immediate impact. *Working With Difficult and Resistant Staff* makes extensive use of bullet points, checklists, and brief descriptions in assisting principals to learn and use the information. Each chapter ends with questions to help readers review and reflect on the material that has been discussed. We also include many exercises and templates that have been designed for principals to use in their planning as they work to address the difficult or resistant people in their buildings.

Finally, we include many stories illustrating the main points being addressed. These stories are all true and are based on our experiences and those of other principals with whom we have worked over the years. In presenting these stories, we have made some changes to ensure the anonymity of those involved in the original situations. We provide the stories to assist the learning of those who are using this book to gain skills and strategies to improve their work with difficult or resistant staff members.

Putting together all of the skills you learn in this book will enable you to identify, confront, and manage all of the difficult and resistant people you encounter. The various people we have worked with over the years have found it liberating to implement these skills and take control of their schools. As you read the information contained in this book, think about the approaches that specifically fit you and the needs of your school. First, try out those ideas that are most comfortable for you to implement, and then try out new ideas that are outside of your comfort zone as you build the expectations for good program implementation.

We wish you well as you implement these ideas. You *will* see an improvement in your skills as you deal with difficult and resistant people.

How Did They Get This Way?

Wanda, a high school principal, is working with her math teachers to help them develop courses that will enable students from diverse backgrounds to be more successful in math and move into higher-level courses. Jerry, the department chair and a veteran teacher, is opposed to refining the courses and views the process as threatening to his leadership. After all, for the past twenty years, the way they have been teaching math at Normal High School has worked for most of the students. The teachers who have been at the school the longest have earned the right to teach the more advanced sections, while new teachers need to prove themselves by teaching the more challenging students. Jerry openly opposes the changes and bullies the rest of the department members into going along with his ideas.

About halfway through the semester, several of the other math teachers start to talk to Wanda about their discomfort with how Jerry is running the department and tell her that not all of the math teachers share his opinions. They want to look at the new ideas Wanda is proposing but are afraid to challenge Jerry on his views. Wanda thinks about the situation and decides that she needs to deal directly with Jerry to try to understand his perspective and work with him to hopefully move the project forward.

She thinks through the meeting and puts strategies in place to ensure that it will be productive. She opens by asking, "Jerry, can you outline your reservations about the changes I've proposed?" He rambles on for about ten minutes about how the proposed curriculum will change the department and get in the way of its successful record of helping the top-end students achieve. As Jerry vents, Wanda listens and writes notes summarizing his major points. She periodically reflects back those points and makes sure she tries to listen and understand his objections to the new ideas.

"It's about time someone listened to me," Jerry finally says with relief. "In all my years in the department, I have been the sole advocate for high expectations for math students in the school."

As she listens, Wanda begins to understand some of the history of change at the school and how Jerry had been involved in negative experiences in the past. She states what she has learned about him: "You have had negative experiences with change in the past." And then she asks, "What problems do you think we need to talk about in order to avoid making the same mistakes that you had to deal with in past change efforts?"

Jerry quickly replies, "It's about time we talked about this." As Wanda continues to talk with Jerry about his past experiences, she discovers that he had been eager to look at new ideas earlier in his career but had gotten into trouble with his colleagues and the board during an initiative that he had supported. He tells Wanda that they had underestimated parental concerns about the new program. The parents had gone to the board, and the administration had not supported Jerry as he was attacked by his colleagues and several board members. He had vowed that he would never put himself in a position where he would be criticized again.

Wanda finally understands why Jerry has a negative attitude toward change. She decides that she needs to spend more time with him and try to understand more about his past experiences. Now that she understands why Jerry is concerned and how he got that way, she is able to meet with him and periodically talk through his concerns. She is able to move the project forward step by step because she uses her knowledge of what had made Jerry skeptical of new ideas and change in the past.

This story demonstrates the importance of finding out and understanding how the difficult or resistant staff members you are dealing with got that way. When you know the source of the resistance or difficulty, you have a better idea of how to respond or how to head off a potential problem.

The Impact of Life Experiences on Mindsets and Behaviors

Each of us has undertaken a unique journey to get to the current point in our lives. This journey has had an impact on our personality and behaviors. In the example we just gave, Wanda took the time to find out why Jerry had developed his attitude toward change and new ideas. Once she understood where he was coming from, she was better able to reflect on a plan to help him move from where he was to a place closer to where he needed to be to begin to accept the change that she was advocating.

In our work with difficult and resistant people, we have found it valuable to use a framework or model to understand how they developed their thought processes. We have seen people go through the following stages as they develop their knowledge and attitudes (Eller & Eller, 2009):

1 A person experiences a series of events. Her mind takes in the information or data from these experiences.

2 The person begins to see the common attributes of these experiences and the information drawn from them. She starts to put together the information and draw conclusions about the experiences.

3 These conclusions begin to form definite patterns. The patterns work together to become a way of thinking or *frame of reference* for the person. This frame of reference begins to govern the way she sees the world and becomes reality for her.

4 The frame of reference establishes a comfort zone for the person. Experiences and information that fit into this frame of reference reinforce her thought pattern. She becomes comfortable in her existing thought pattern because it provides predictability. Incoming information is filtered through this frame of reference. Information that matches the frame is accepted; information that conflicts with it can be discounted.

5 Over time, the living or work environment can change. The person becomes uncomfortable with the new environment because it doesn't fit her frame of reference. To remain comfortable and reinforce the old thought pattern, she may change or discount the information being provided in the new environment.

6 Because the person is trying to fit the new information from the environment into an old frame of reference, she can become resistant to the new thought patterns, behaviors, or information coming to her.

7 After exposure to the new information for a period of time, the person begins to see how it connects or is related to her original frame of reference. The new incoming information begins to assist her as she develops a new frame of reference. Over time, she is able to embrace the new ideas and integrate them into her operating procedures.

So, if one of the major functions of the human brain is to identify and develop patterns using the information it gathers, it is natural that the people working in our schools will construct their own beliefs and behaviors based on their experiences. As you think about your work with difficult and resistant staff members, it's important to consider some of the possible origins of their negative behavior.

Administrators' Frames of Reference

Just as frames of reference can influence and shape the thought patterns of teachers, they can affect us as leaders. Because we can have a definite way of thinking about issues, we ourselves may be resistant to new ideas and strategies or make rash judgments about teacher behaviors. Our own resistant thinking might cause us to act in the following ways:

- Hanging on to preconceived thoughts and misconceptions about staff members

- Remaining focused on staff members' past issues or behaviors without allowing them a chance to change

- Attaching negative thoughts to a person because of his or her association with other negative staff members

- Developing an opinion about a person's attitude or competency because of his or her background

As the building leader, you need to examine your thoughts about your staff members to ensure that your interactions with and decisions about them are not tainted by your own frames of reference. You must be able to keep an open mind in dealing with your staff members. An exercise we call "Understanding Why Others May Be Difficult" will help you identify and understand the background behind the difficult and resistant behaviors you may see in your school. Visit **go.solution-tree.com/leadership** to download this exercise.

Responses to Chaos and Conflict

When people are introduced to new ideas or changes, they can have varying responses. Some look forward to new things and embrace change, while others like their environment to be regular and predictable. The latter hold the potential to become difficult or resistant in light of the change. Some people feel they lose control of a situation when a change occurs, and this loss of control can lead to a feeling of chaos.

Chaos

Chaos is a state of unpredictability and uncertainty. All groups and individuals have to go through some degree of chaos periodically in order to rejuvenate and change. Chaos can be associated with a new job assignment, a change in the established curriculum, or a new supervisor. Chaos can also involve a more major change, such as losing a job, moving to a new location, or experiencing the death of a family member or close friend. All of these chaotic events can force us to redefine ourselves and in some cases reinvent what we do. For some people, chaos is a natural part of life and doesn't have much of an impact, while for others, it can turn their entire world upside down.

Because of the intense emotions that can be associated with chaos, it is something we need to pay close attention to as leaders. As we approach new programs or initiatives, we need to be careful to monitor them closely to make sure staff members do not experience levels of chaos that are too high. It is helpful to hold regular meetings with the staff, especially during the initial stages of a new program, to assess the level of chaos and help staff members work through it. It is also helpful to meet with staff members individually during the initial stages of a project to assess the level of chaos they are personally experiencing.

Conflict

Conflict occurs naturally in most organizations and groups as individuals encounter differences of opinion related to their perspectives and experiences. If you are implementing new programs, making changes in your school, or taking on difficult or resistant people, you will experience conflict. In this section, we will talk about two kinds of conflict normally present in school settings and their impact on the school environment.

Substantive Conflict

When individuals or groups of people encounter differences of opinion or disagree over issues related to philosophy, values, or belief, they are engaged in *substantive conflict*. Substantive conflict can actually be good for your school and the people working there. In our work with schools, we have seen substantive conflict on a very regular basis. It can be healthy for groups to openly discuss their philosophies, values, and beliefs. The typical problem that school staff members face is that they do not have the skills or support to engage in healthy conversations related to substantive conflict. When groups engage in conversations without the structures needed to successfully understand each other's perspectives and to productively work through conflict toward mutual understanding, their conflict can move away from substantive to affective.

Affective Conflict

Affective conflict relates to personal disagreements. When groups lack the foundation or skills needed to have open conversations about their philosophies, values, or beliefs, they move toward a more defensive mode. In our experience, the conflict moves away from a content-based mode and toward a more personality-based mode. When conflict turns personal, it can cause people to become difficult and resistant because of the need to either win the fight or defend themselves personally. They will naturally attack rather than have a healthy debate over the issue.

When leaders encounter conflict situations in groups, it is important that they be able to label them as either affective or substantive. Table I.1 provides a brief outline for you to follow in identifying these two types of conflict.

Table I.1: Types of Conflict

Substantive	Affective
The focus is on issues related to philosophies, values, beliefs, processes, or goals.	The focus is on issues related to the people or the personalities involved in a conversation.
Substantive conflict can help a team improve its functioning because members learn how to work through issues.	Affective conflict negatively impacts working relationships.
Teams engaged in substantive conflict tend to use more information and be more reflective in making their decision. This is due, in part, to the fact that team members debate the idea rather than the personality.	Teams experiencing affective conflict tend to make decisions using less information so that they can move on from the conflict situation.

Understanding conflict types is important in managing difficult or resistant people. Some people have experienced only affective conflict and have developed defense mechanisms to protect themselves from attack. At times, these defense mechanisms become too harsh or negative. If you understand this concept, you can structure meetings and other interactions so that individuals and groups learn they do not need to put up defense mechanisms in order to debate issues. This gives them a chance to lower their defenses and become less difficult or resistant.

Winners and Losers in the Change

In any change effort, some people are going to "win," while others will "lose." When we say that people will win, we mean that their personal or professional lives will be better as a result of the change you are introducing. Those people who will lose as a result of the change may experience (or feel they have experienced) a decrease in the quality of their personal or professional life. We understand that this explanation is simple, but it illustrates the importance of working to understand the balance sheet of wins and losses, because people who lose in a change initiative tend to become difficult and resistant. Table I.2 lists some of the typical wins and losses that are associated with change.

Table I.2: Wins and Losses Associated With Organizational Change

Win	Loss
An increase of power within the organization	A decrease of power within the organization
A perceived increase in intellectual power, especially if the employee's idea is accepted in the organization	A perceived decrease in intellectual power, especially if the employee's idea is not accepted in the organization
An easier workload if the new idea fits the employee's established strengths	A more difficult workload if the new idea requires learning new work behaviors
A feeling of favor within the organization because the employee's idea was implemented by the leadership	A feeling of disfavor within the organization because the employee's idea was not implemented by the leadership

As a leader, it's important to be able to examine a planned change in terms of the potential wins and losses that could result from its implementation. You should make a written tally of them so that you can easily see whether the wins outweigh the losses. You should also connect every potential win and loss with the names of the staff members who will most likely experience it. By determining who could stand to lose the most, you may be able to intervene early on to ensure that they do not become difficult or resistant. Visit **go.solution-tree.com/leadership** to download a "Wins and Losses Diagnostic Template" and a "Winners and Losers T-Chart."

Lack of Knowledge About the Change

People can also become difficult and resistant when they feel they don't have enough information about the new idea or change to be able to predict what will happen as a result of its implementation. Because they can pinpoint a lack of information as the cause of their negative feelings about the change, they don't experience the more overwhelming anxiety associated with chaos. But it's still important for you as a leader to recognize their discomfort as a problem and to try to reduce or eliminate ambiguity when implementing new ideas or change.

Poorly Managed Transitions

With any change, the old way of doing things will end. We often forget about this important aspect of the change process. In many cases, the transition from existing to future is not designed or handled well. If some of your staff members have been the targets of community outcry or have felt the effects of whole-school anxiety as a result of poorly managed transitions during previous change efforts, it's no wonder that they are now difficult and resistant. As you manage change, be aware of these transitional stages. Effective principals guide their staff members through the process of "letting go" of the old ways of doing business.

Faulty Change Management in Previous Situations

Mismanagement can be specific to transitions, or it can characterize the entire change process. Faulty change management can include poor planning, giving teachers and other stakeholders limited information about the change, providing inadequate resources for the change, and failing to build a support group for the new idea or change. Poorly managed change efforts can breed difficult and resistant staff members. If staff members have endured faulty change management in past programs or initiatives, they will remember their negative experiences and resist your new efforts as well. Assessing previous change efforts to find out the level of support—if any—these people received can be helpful to you as you begin to understand their perspective and develop strategies to productively work with them.

Summary

In this introduction, you have learned about some of the situations and conditions that can contribute to making people difficult or resistant. Armed with this important information, you should be able to plan and monitor conditions to minimize difficulties and maximize your success with new projects or changes in procedures.

Understanding some of the factors that may be causing people to be difficult or resistant is an important foundation to have as a leader, but knowing what to do to deal with such people is even more important. In the following chapters, we will offer specific insights and strategies to help you understand and deal with eight types of difficult people that you may encounter:

1　The Underminers

2　The Contrarians

Questions for Reflection

Identify two or three of the most difficult and resistant people on your staff. What might be some of the background or reasons that helped make them so negative? How might you use this information to work with them in a more positive or productive manner in the future?

What does the concept of "winners and losers" have to do with difficult and resistant people? How does knowing this information help you possibly prevent issues from emerging in the first place?

What are some of the past experiences of your difficult and resistant staff members that could be contributing to their attitudes? If these experiences are not evident, how might you do some research to find them?

Why is it important to understand how people could have become difficult and resistant?

chapter 1

The Underminers

In almost every school, a personality type exists that can threaten the climate and culture of trust and slow down implementation efforts. We call this type "the Underminer." While Underminers' exact behaviors can be variable, in general they act supportive in your presence but make negative comments about you or the school behind your back.

As you read this chapter, you will learn the following:

- Typical behaviors of Underminers
- Strategies for handling Underminers
- The principal's role in creating Underminers
- Ways to help develop the skills of other staff members to effectively deal with Underminers in their midst

Behaviors of Underminers

Here are some of the specific behaviors that are typical of Underminers:

- Agreeing with you in your presence but criticizing the program or implementation behind your back
- Sitting in a meeting and not sharing any comments or feedback but organizing or engaging in negative conversations in the hall, lounge, and parking lot
- Telling you they will try the new idea or strategy in their classroom but failing to follow through or even attempting to sabotage the effort
- Working to stir up negative sentiment against the change or new idea

Underminers are particularly difficult to deal with because of the power they can have over the other staff members. They are good at expressing some of the reservations that other staff members may be thinking but don't have the courage to say out loud. They also create fear in others because their behavior can go beyond just being negative about the change or new idea. They might work to undermine *anyone* who is positive about the change. This behavior can cause problems as Underminers try to shift the power balance and recruit other negative staff members.

Let's see how one principal handles a small group of Underminers who threaten to derail a school improvement project.

Scenario: We Don't Believe It

At Hughes Middle School, the principal, Scott, calls a meeting to share some bad news about the latest student achievement results. It seems that even though the school updated both the language arts and math curricular areas, purchased new materials, and provided professional development for teachers during the last three years, the results of the latest state assessments show that HMS students are still lagging behind their peer groups in these areas. Scott has decided that something needs to be done to examine and remedy this situation. As he presents this information, he tells the staff he wants to wait for comments until the end of the presentation. He also shares that he is planning to involve the school improvement team in looking at the data and reacting to his ideas for improvement.

Scott asks the staff members if they have any comments or questions about the issue and his proposal to begin to address the situation. Several staff members say that they think his plan has merit and that they support it. Many don't state their opinions.

After the meeting, Scott notices clusters of teachers gathering in class-rooms and in the school parking lot to share their real feelings about the situation. When he approaches these groups, the conversations stop. Over the next couple of days, Scott begins to hear from teachers and some members of his school improvement team that three to four teachers are complaining about the plan and Scott's leadership on the issue. Scott decides that he has to address this situation and get the concerns out into the open.

Lessons From This Scenario

Scott needs to find ways to confront the negativity of the situation, ensure that everyone understands the truth behind the situation, and provide a way for people to get their feelings out on the table. Here are a few approaches that Scott could take to deal with the scenario:

- Scott could call a follow-up meeting of the entire staff and tell the staff members that he realizes that his announcement the other day might have taken people by surprise. In the previous meeting, he had not planned for their need to express their concerns. In this meeting, he could hand out sheets of paper and ask them to write down their concerns. Once they had done so, he could collect the papers and—if he thought the negative energy was too strong to open up a conversation about them—tabulate the concerns. Then, in a second follow-up meeting, he could hand out a list of compiled concerns and hold an open discussion about them.

- Scott could call a follow-up meeting and, using the format just described, ask the staff members to write down their concerns. Once they had done so, he could ask them to meet in small groups of three to four to talk through the issues related to his announcement at the first meeting. As they were talking in small groups, Scott could walk around the room and check in on their conversations. Walking around would give him an opportunity to assess the level of negativity or anxiety so that he would be prepared for the next phase of the conversation, when he would ask the staff members to openly discuss their feelings about his announcement.

- After he noticed the parking lot conversations, Scott could engage in informal conversations with faculty members about his announcement. He might want to talk first with the unofficial, stable leaders on the staff and then move on to others. Talking informally with staff members would provide a personal touch and let the staff members know he cared about their concerns related to his announcement.

- If he could isolate those staff members he suspected were spreading the negative energy of undermining, Scott could talk with them individually about their perceptions and concerns. He would need to keep these conversations focused so that the Underminers he talked to wouldn't perceive that he was trying to single them out. He would also want to let them know that they could talk about their concerns without fear of retribution.

Further Strategies for Handling Underminers

Trying to deal with undermining behavior is highly situational. When determining the proper intervention, it is important to consider the power and credibility of the Underminers, as well as the ability of your school culture to handle bringing the conflict into the open. Here are some strategies that can be effective both in dealing directly with the Underminers and in developing a culture of open communication:

- Stand up to Underminers. If you suspect that someone is undermining you and you can find evidence to back up your assertion, confront the person. Plan your conference to include your evidence, a strategy to get the other person's side of the story, a directive to stop his or her negative behavior, and a recommendation for an alternative way for him or her to share concerns with you. If you don't confront Underminers and their behavior, it may go on unchecked.

- Model appropriate behaviors as a leader. Staff members take note of what you do as well as what you say. They look to you to model the proper behaviors in handling situations that arise. If you want people to feel comfortable sharing their concerns, you need to communicate and show them that you value their opinions (whether or not they agree with you). If you have concerns about an individual, share them with that person rather than tell everyone else on the staff. You should model integrity rather than secretive behaviors. Make sure that all staff members receive the information they need in order to do their jobs properly. If you make mistakes, let people know that, and tell them what you plan to do to correct them. Model openness and listening, and your staff will soon follow suit.

- Seek to develop trust with employees so they will feel comfortable sharing their concerns with you. The following actions will help to establish trust:

  - Meet privately with individuals to get their opinions about ideas and strategies.

  - Listen as employees share ideas; use reflecting statements (see pages 23–24) to help clarify rather than judge.

  - Write down ideas as they are shared with you.

  - Thank staff members for sharing their thoughts.

- Let people know that you know there are issues with the new idea or strategy.

- Provide opportunities for people to voice their opinions openly without retribution.

The Principal's Role in Creating Underminers

At times, Underminers are made, not born. If principals are not careful and observant, they can create or strengthen the presence of Underminers on their staff. In this section, we will look at some of the common ways this happens and suggest the appropriate counterstrategies.

- Running buildings in an autocratic manner—When principals don't allow staff members to give input or to participate in decisions, people will take their opinions underground. Be careful about how you run your building. Be sure to give staff members opportunities to offer suggestions, and include them in the decision-making process when appropriate. Usually, the best way to gather their input is through structured activities.

- Failing to explain the reasons behind change initiatives—When people do not understand the reasons behind decisions, they will question the decisions with their peers. Over time, these discussions can turn into undermining. Be sure to provide the rationale for your ideas and initiatives. The rationale should be based on actual situations or needs that you have found in your building operations.

- Punishing staff members who question or disagree with their opinions—By setting negative consequences for disagreement, principals can drive questioning people underground to avoid punishment. This will breed Underminers on a staff. As your faculty members discuss potential changes or decisions, be sure to build in opportunities for them to provide appropriate counterarguments. This debate should be conducted in a structured manner and appear to be a natural part of the process. Simply asking teams to generate what they perceive as the pros and cons of an idea will positively reinforce appropriate debate and will ensure that the faculty examines all sides of an issue before making a decision.

- Giving negative people positive reinforcement or more professional opportunities—Sometimes, principals will try to reduce negativity by giving the difficult staff members more attention and professional opportunities. This behavior usually has the opposite effect and breeds more negativity and discontent among staff members. Underminers thrive in this type of environment. Carefully consider the assignments you give people. Be sure that only your positive staff members receive any assignments that carry a major leadership responsibility or that have the potential for influence over others.

These are just a few ways in which principals can unknowingly develop Underminers on their staff. Watch your behaviors and the staff's reaction to them. If you mentally step back and examine your behaviors, you may be able to prevent staff members from resorting to undermining.

Working With Staff Members to Deal With Underminers

The most effective way to counter the behavior of Underminers is to establish a culture of open communication, in which staff members are encouraged to voice their opinions and share their concerns in appropriate, tactful ways. Such a culture reduces the likelihood that staff members will resort to undermining behaviors in the first place. But in the event that undermining occurs, having good communication strategies in place will allow you and your staff to work together to deal with the problem.

In this section, we will present strategies for developing healthy communication in general and then close with specific strategies for helping your staff members address undermining behaviors.

Private Concerns

At times, people find it difficult to express their concerns about an idea or an implementation. Consider providing a suggestion box or concerns box that allows staff members to pose questions or share concerns anonymously. Once you have collected some suggestions, you may want to report them out or share a compiled list at a staff meeting.

"Tip the Scales" Activity

When looking at a new idea or implementation, it's important to hold various conversations to help people develop a frame of reference around the new plan. The "Tip the Scales" activity is good to start with because it allows the open discussion of what people see as the potential benefits and drawbacks of a change. It works like this:

- On a large piece of chart paper, draw a scale similar to the one shown in figure 1.1.

- Describe the change or new idea to the staff.

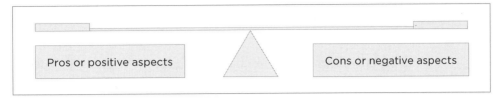

Figure 1.1: "Tip the Scales" chart.

- Ask staff members to write positive and negative aspects of the change (if implemented) on sticky notes. They should complete these sticky notes privately.

- After all staff members have had a chance to complete their sticky notes, ask them to post them on the scale drawn on the chart paper, placing the positive aspects on the positive side and the negative aspects on the negative side. You may want to keep this step anonymous as well. You could collect all of the notes from the staff and then put them up on the chart, or you could leave the room and ask the staff members to post their notes. In some instances, it might be adequate for you just to walk to the back of the room and let your staff post the notes. Use the strategy that will be most comfortable for your staff and that will maintain the anonymous nature of the comments.

- Hold a conversation about what people learned as a result of the activity. Talk about how you can work together as a staff to overcome the negative aspects of the new idea or strategy.

Pro-Con Conversation

A strategy that is similar to the Tip the Scales activity and that encourages staff members to express their concerns is called a Pro-Con Conversation. Here is how it works:

- As the leader of the group, provide ample time on the agenda for the conversation (thirty to forty-five minutes).

- Let group members know that they will be talking through the new idea or implementation. Make a large chart with two columns, one labeled "Pros" and one labeled "Cons." In this conversation you want the staff members to address the following topics:

    - The specifics of the new idea or strategy and their understanding of them

- - The potentially positive aspects of the new idea or implementation

  - The potentially negative or challenging aspects of the new idea or change; concerns about the change

- Keep the group within each of the topics until it is clearly understood and they have explored all the ideas within it.

- Once the first three topics have been explored, move the group into the last one, "What will we need, or what do we need to do, to overcome the challenges?"

- Post the results of the discussion in the lounge or workroom to give people a chance to reflect on their work. Revisit the concepts at the next staff meeting, and make some decisions around the new idea or implementation.

Figure 1.2 is a planning guide for conducting a Pro-Con Conversation.

Group Norms

If staff members are going to be discussing sensitive issues, it is helpful to develop group norms that stress honesty and healthy communication and

---

Pro-Con Conversation Planning Guide

The Pro-Con Conversation is a good strategy to help everyone clearly understand a new idea or implementation and its potential impacts. In holding this type of conversation, you want to take people through the process step by step to ensure that they are able to understand the details of the new idea or implementation and have an open conversation about its pros and cons. Use this planning guide to help you conduct such a conversation.

1. Display a large chart with two columns, one labeled "Pros" and one labeled "Cons."

2. Identify the details or specifics of this change or new idea. What is it? What does it involve? What will it look like when it is implemented or completed?

3. Consider the pros of the idea or implementation. What are the positives or advantages if we implement this new idea or strategy?

4. Consider the cons of or concerns about the idea or implementation. What are the negative aspects or concerns associated with implementing this new idea?

5. Consider the needs or strategies to overcome the challenges. What will we need, or what do we need to do, to overcome the challenges presented to us by this new idea?

Figure 1.2: Steps of a Pro-Con Conversation.

problem-solving processes. You can lead this effort by speaking to the staff about the importance of honesty and collaborative problem solving and then asking staff members to discuss how they want to approach their work together. A finished norm might look like this:

> Our group will be open and honest with each other when we have concerns. We will be tactful but share our concerns honestly.

Once your group has settled on its norms, help to ensure that they are followed between parties and among the whole staff at the school. Revisit the norms at faculty meetings, and ask everyone to talk about how they are being followed and what impact they are having on the school. The group should make adjustments to the norms when it is apparent that they need to be refined.

If the staff does not have the capacity to develop a norm for honesty and collaborative problem solving, develop a ground rule and share it with the staff. A ground rule is a parameter established by a leader or a person outside of the immediate group. Ground rules are good because they cause quick compliance. They do not usually involve the commitment of the group members, so there may be a challenge in getting group compliance with a ground rule. An effective ground rule for sharing concerns might look like this:

> If a staff member has a concern, he or she must communicate directly with the source of the concern before talking to anyone else.

As with norms, the leader will need to follow up with the group regarding its progress with the implementation of a ground rule.

Open Communication and Dealing With Underminers

Even though it may seem obvious, some staff members may have difficulty recognizing negative, undermining behaviors in their colleagues. Conduct sessions at staff meetings in which you talk about—and model—integrity and open communication about concerns. Contrast this with the ways that Underminers operate. Point out the destructive nature of undermining, and stress that the staff needs to work together to prevent it or to deal with it when it happens at the school.

Acknowledge that it is tempting to follow the lead of others when they are complaining behind someone's back. Then teach your staff how to resist this potentially destructive and disabling behavior. Here are some strategies that staff members can use:

- Encourage Underminers to take their issues to the source.
- Confront the Underminer's behavior:

- Ask the Underminer for clear examples; drive him or her to be specific.

- Ask the Underminer to provide reasons and rationales for his or her assertions.

- Ignore or refuse to be influenced by the undermining behavior.

Be proactive, and make resistance to undermining an operating norm for your school.

Summary

In this chapter, we have looked at a group of difficult and resistant staff members who can threaten your school culture and undermine your efforts to improve the school. The undermining behavior not only affects you as a leader but also sets the stage for this kind of behavior to become the norm in your school. Once people begin to sense the loss of honesty and integrity, they can become less invested in the success of the school and in the interdependent relationships with other staff members that are so crucial for their success. In extreme cases, the more positive staff members choose to leave such negative environments and work where they are more supported. When you lose the positive people, the proportion of negative people increases, making it even more difficult for everyone to work together as a staff.

Questions for Reflection

How can developing a pro-con list help diminish behind-the-scenes complaining and venting?

What are some of the ways that you can unknowingly strengthen the influence of Underminers on your staff? How can you minimize their development?

Why is it important to engage the rest of the staff in combating the difficulty caused by Underminers?

What are some strategies that you can use to help the rest of the staff engage in reducing the influence of these Underminers?

chapter 2

The Contrarians

There is a group of people who seem to embrace conflict and always want to argue. No matter what is suggested, these people have a counterpoint. We call them "the Contrarians." Contrarians not only like to disagree a lot, they also make others uncomfortable and reluctant to engage in moving forward on school improvement initiatives.

As you read this chapter, you will learn the following:

- The traits of Contrarians

- Strategies for dealing with Contrarians

- The principal's role in creating Contrarians

- Ways to help your school staff work with Contrarians

Traits of Contrarians

Contrarians are openly aggressive and challenging. Here are some of their common traits:

- A readiness and an ability to fight with and confront others with little advance preparation

- A belief that if they don't disagree with someone else, they will be perceived as *totally* agreeing and compromising their own position

- A good basic knowledge of a variety of topics—Sometimes Contrarians possess incorrect knowledge but still profess to know a lot about the topic at hand.

- The ability to ignore the opinions and logic of others while arguing their own points

- An egocentric focus and a lack of caring about how others perceive them
- The ability to get energized as a result of the argument—This energy seems to increase as the confrontation gets stronger.

Let's see how one principal handles a staff member who is intent on undermining his initiatives.

Scenario: I'm Right, and Everyone Else Needs to Know It

Matt is a first-year principal at Armstrong Middle School. He is holding his second meeting with the entire staff. As Matt is explaining some of the new procedures that are being implemented under his leadership, one of his teachers, Tammy, stands up and wants to share her thoughts about them. Matt decides to signal to Tammy to sit down while he continues the meeting. At the end of the meeting, Matt asks to meet with her.

During their private meeting, Tammy wants to know why he is making changes. She raises her voice frequently and tries to intimidate him. Matt tells her that the new procedures are not going to change, and he expects her to follow them.

The following day, Tammy asks to meet with Matt again. Matt thinks about several things before he meets with her. He decides to have the meeting in his office at the table. He makes sure he is mentally prepared for the meeting. When they meet, Tammy tells him that she wants him to rethink the changes that he has put in place. Matt informs her that these changes were made after meeting with the building leadership team and after meeting with all staff members in the summer. He tells her that he knows change is hard, but he wants her to try to move forward and implement the changes.

Matt learns that during her lunchtime, she is still trying to complain to other staff members about the changes. He decides that he cannot allow her to be negative. Matt meets with her and tells her that he needs her to be more positive and that the other staff members are tired of her being negative. She is surprised to hear that the staff members think she is negative. No one has ever told her she was negative. Matt asks her if that is how she wants to be perceived. She tells Matt that she probably needs to make a building change or some kind of change in her life outside of school. Matt tells her that this is a new beginning for the whole school and that everyone deserves an opportunity to change.

Lessons From This Scenario

Matt did a number of things right in his dealings with Tammy but could have benefited from using some additional strategies. Here are our recommendations for possible ways to handle this and similar situations:

- Agree to disagree if issues come up at a meeting. Since Contrarians love to argue and are normally very good at it, don't give them the satisfaction of carrying out a debate with them in front of an audience. Let the Contrarian know that on this point you won't agree, and direct him or her to talk with you about it later. Your statement might sound like this:

  - "Obviously, we aren't going to solve this now. Let's talk after the meeting."

  - "Since we are on different sides of this issue, it won't be resolved today. Let's meet and continue our conversation."

  - "You and I are not on the same page here. Rather than taking everyone's time, we need to schedule a meeting to figure this out later."

- Thank the person for bringing up the idea or objection. Confirm what is accurate in his or her statement, and outline what needs further clarification. This can be done in a group meeting, if appropriate, or through a private conversation. Contrarians need to know they have been heard, so confirming that you heard their message may lower the energy associated with their contrarian behavior.

- Confront the Contrarian in a private meeting, and address the negative behavior. As you think about using this strategy, be well prepared before you schedule the conference. Since Contrarians fight all the time, they are adept at thinking on their feet. You may want to write out your concerns and practice them before actually holding the conference. Do not get caught up in trying to convince the Contrarian that you are right or trying to come to agreement. The purpose of the conference is just to let the Contrarian know you have a concern.

- Use content-reflecting statements and emotion-reflecting statements to let the Contrarian know that you are listening to and understand what he or she is trying to say. Once you communicate your receptiveness and understanding, the Contrarian will be more willing to listen to you. Figure 2.1 (page 24) gives examples of each kind of reflecting statement.

- Provide a directive to the Contrarian to stop the behavior.
- Document the Contrarian's behavior for further disciplinary action.

Content Reflecting

When using content reflecting, you are attempting to demonstrate that you understand what the person is trying to tell you. Content reflecting is fairly straightforward. You repeat back what you heard in slightly different words.

Contrarian statement: "You know, this new idea you are proposing has not been tested or researched. It could be something that will not work here."

Content-reflecting response: "You think the idea could be flawed or have some potential for failure here."

Emotion Reflecting

Sometimes, strong emotions are associated with the comments made by Contrarians. You can reflect back their emotions to communicate that you understand where they are coming from.

Contrarian statement: "I'm surprised and hurt by your statement. You obviously don't understand me."

Emotion-reflecting statement: "You feel hurt and upset by what I said."

Figure 2.1: Content and emotion reflecting.

Further Strategies for Dealing With Contrarians

In order to deal more effectively with Contrarians, you will need to consider a variety of ideas and strategies. We have found that the following strategies have proven effective in dealing with the unique challenges posed by Contrarians.

Framing

Framing is a technique a leader uses to establish boundaries around a conversation. An effective frame constrains the conversation and keeps people on track. Setting boundaries for a conversation is crucial because Contrarians and other types of difficult and resistant people sometimes try to disrupt a meeting by making comments that can take a group off-task. Once the group has been destabilized, the difficult and resistant people win because the group's energy and attention are occupied with the new, off-task topic. We have found the skill of framing to be foundational in our work with administrators confronting the behaviors of difficult and resistant people. However, framing is a good technique to use in working with *all* groups, even if they don't contain such people. Any group will benefit from having boundaries in relation to their meetings.

Framing statements can be simple and direct. Here are some examples you may consider using to help keep meetings on track and to minimize the impact of Contrarians or other difficult people who try to take your group off task:

- "In today's meeting, we will focus on [name the major topics of the meeting]."
- "We need to restrict our agenda today to [name the agenda topics]."
- "As we talk today, I will share with you the details of [name topic]. Once I have outlined the topic, I will share the potential impacts of [name topic]. Finally, I will ask you to meet in small groups and generate your thoughts and ideas."
- "In our meeting, we will be talking about three things: [name them]."
- "Today, we will look at only the first part of [name topic]. In future meetings, we will look at the other parts of [name topic]."

Framing is especially powerful when coupled with other techniques. We will discuss two of those techniques here and return to framing in chapter 8.

Pausing

Framing statements can be reinforced through the use of effective pauses. Pausing your speech places additional emphasis on the element that occurred right before the pause. See how this works in the following examples:

- "Today, we are here to focus on three things. [*Pause.*] First, we will examine your negative behaviors. [*Pause.*] Next, we will look at the impact this has on the rest of the staff. [*Pause.*] And finally, we will develop a plan for you to improve this behavior."
- "In our time together today, I want to address the problems with your behavior at the staff meeting last week. [*Pause.*] I want to give you a chance to share your thoughts for a few minutes. [*Pause.*] Then, I plan to share how I want you to change this behavior in the future."

In both of these examples, the pauses work to emphasize the separate parts of the message the leader wants to deliver.

Recognizing Concerns

In some cases, you can use a framing statement to recognize a Contrarian's concern or perspective without letting him or her take over or dominate the conversation. You can prepare your responses in advance of a meeting by developing these kinds of framing statements:

- A statement that recognizes the Contrarian's concern or perspective—For example: "First, we'll look at the positive aspects of the change, and then we'll move to your concerns."

- A statement that brings the person back to the meeting agenda—For example: "In moving forward, we won't be revisiting past mistakes, we'll only be focusing on solutions."

- A statement that outlines the agenda for the meeting—For example: "As we work together on this problem, first we will _____; then we will _____."

Delivering Difficult Messages

When working with Contrarians, you will eventually need to confront their behavior. Because they are usually highly skilled in controlling conversations, you will need to be armed and ready to confront them. Having an effective plan is the best insurance for maintaining control of the conversation. For your message to have an impact, you need to be able to use the following strategies:

- Eye contact—Eye contact is an important part of success in confronting Contrarians. When you can look someone in the eye, it conveys confidence and authority and puts you in control of the conversation.

- Specificity/clarity—A common behavior that we see in supervisors who are first learning a new communication skill is that they talk around the issue. Beating around the bush can convey a lack of confidence in addressing a situation. When confronting Contrarians, it's important that you state your concerns as clearly and concisely as possible. As their supervisor, you are expected to be able to label inappropriate behaviors and share clear expectations. Be clear and direct, and you will be much better prepared to handle Contrarian conferences.

- Authority voice—Another strategy that we have found helpful in working with Contrarians is authority voice. The literature about voice power and our own observations of effective leaders have revealed that people in positions of authority tend to lower the pitch of their voice at the end of a statement or directive. Walter Cronkite, the late news anchor, offered a prime example of this principle in his delivery. For years he ended his newscasts with the statement "And that's the way it is." If you listen carefully to the pitch of his voice, it goes down at the end of the statement. While this is a hard concept to demonstrate in print, it is fairly easy to incorporate into your speech. As you deliver a directive, just slightly lower your chin at the end of the statement. This will cause your vocal cords to loosen and produce a lower pitch. The person hearing your directive will subconsciously pick up the lower pitch and perceive you as an authority figure.

Planning the Meeting

As we mentioned earlier, because Contrarians are so good at thinking on their feet and gaining control of a conversation, it is advisable to create a detailed plan for the private conference in which you will confront the negative behaviors. Here are the steps you should plan to follow:

1 Design a statement to set the proper tone for the conference.

2 Outline what will be talked about at the meeting. Frame the boundaries of the conversation, how you plan to move forward, and the role you want the Contrarian to play in the conference.

3 Tell the Contrarian your issue or concern and why this situation is an issue or concern. Feel free to share how you think it is negatively impacting the school or the other staff members.

4 Tell the Contrarian that the negative or distracting behavior needs to stop immediately. Provide a timeline for the behavior to stop if you feel a transition plan needs to be put into place.

5 Make sure that the Contrarian understands what you are directing him or her to do. Don't worry about agreement with your directive. Instead, focus on the Contrarian's understanding of the directive.

6 Tell the Contrarian that you will be checking to make sure the issue has been addressed and taken care of. Make sure he or she understands that you are serious and will follow up to make sure your concerns have been addressed.

7 Thank the Contrarian for taking care of the issue and for talking with you at this meeting.

Here is an example of how your part of the conference would sound if you followed this plan:

> Thank you for taking the time to meet with me today so we can address my concerns over your behavior here on the faculty.
>
> During this conference, I plan to outline my concerns with your behavior. Once that has been done, I'll let you share your perspective. Finally, we will come up with a plan to ensure this type of thing does not happen again.
>
> At the last faculty meeting, you attacked Ben for his idea without listening to it completely. This caused Ben to become defensive and others on the faculty to shut down and not share their ideas. This has happened at other meetings, but I chose to overlook it temporarily. We can't have this type of behavior at our staff meetings.
>
> In the future, you need to follow the group norms we developed as a faculty to govern how we disagree with each other. You need to stop confronting others and follow the norms.
>
> Please summarize what I want you to do in the future and how we will work together to make it happen.
>
> I plan to follow up with you on a monthly basis, check your concerns, and provide you with ongoing guidance in following the group norms.
>
> Thank you for meeting with me and handling this situation in a professional manner.

The Principal's Role in Creating Contrarians

Principals can inadvertently reinforce or develop the behavior of Contrarians. In this section, we will look at some of the common ways they do so and suggest the appropriate counterstrategies.

- Appearing weak in their leadership—If a principal is too receptive to negative comments or does not provide a good structure for disagreement, Contrarians can be openly confrontational. Provide the proper context and vehicles for dissonant comments.

- Not carefully thinking through their ideas before presenting them to their staff members at a meeting—If a principal appears tentative in his or her delivery of ideas or suggestions, Contrarians can pick up on this and seek the opportunity to confront the principal. Be prepared when presenting ideas to your staff members.

- Failing to build informal leadership support for ideas and initiatives—When there is limited support for ideas and initiatives among the informal leaders on the staff, Contrarians may choose to take advantage of the situation. Before announcing your ideas or initiatives, always talk through them with the informal building leaders to get their support. Contrarians will be less likely to initiate counterstatements if they know an idea has informal leadership support.

- Hiring Contrarians—Principals may not know how to pick up on signs that a potential hire is a Contrarian. If you begin to notice that the person you are considering seems too confident or talks negatively about his or her present boss or work environment, be careful.

Working With Staff Members to Deal With Contrarians

All staff members need to be aware of the destructiveness of Contrarian behaviors. Conduct sessions at staff meetings in which you talk through the damaging effects that confronting another person can cause. Then help the staff members find ways to work together to prevent Contrarian behavior or deal with it when it occurs.

Group Norms

As is the case when dealing with any type of difficult or resistant behavior, open communication is key. You should work with staff members to set clear operating norms that outline positive ways for people to communicate and to understand one another's perspectives. An example of a group norm that is intended to prevent Contrarian behavior would be:

> When questioning or examining suggestions or ideas, we will use positive processes that maintain the dignity of the person suggesting them.

If the staff lacks the confidence or skills to develop group norms, you might want to set your own ground rules for conversations. A statement that prevents or limits Contrarian behavior might sound like this:

> No one will confront a person making suggestions or sharing ideas in a public meeting or forum.

Problem-Solving Process

If two staff members become involved in a conflict—especially if one of them is a Contrarian—you can show them how to work through their issues by using a systematic problem-solving process. Figure 2.2 outlines the steps you will use to guide staff members through this process.

Problem-Solving Process

If you find that a Contrarian and another staff member have "locked horns" on an issue, you may need to intervene to provide stability for the situation. When you intervene, you are not trying to prove one person right and the other wrong; you are just trying to remove some of the negative energy associated with the situation. Use the following steps to help staff members resolve their conflict:

1. Call the two opposing parties together for a meeting.

2. At the beginning of the meeting, let both parties know that the deadlock is unacceptable and that you want to help them try to work through their differences.

3. Establish the following ground rules for the conversation:

   - During the conference, all parties will keep their voices at a conversational level.

   - While one person is talking, everyone else needs to listen. After that person shares, there will be a time for clarification if needed.

   - The person speaking can share the situation only from his or her perspective. There will be no accusations or assumptions expressed during the conversation.

4. Let the non-Contrarian talk first. Allow this person to lay out the major issues from his or her perspective.

5. Once this person has spoken, ask the other person if he or she needs anything to be clarified. Requests for clarification should be phrased as questions.

6. Allow the Contrarian to share his or her perspective on the situation. Once the Contrarian finishes, allow a time for clarification.

7. Once both parties have spoken, ask them if they need any details to be repeated or clarified. If they do not, ask both parties to share what they are willing to do in order to move forward on the situation. You are not trying to get either party to accept the other's ideas or perspective at this point.

8. If you feel you have a clear understanding of what each party is willing to do to move forward, and you are satisfied with the resolution, develop a plan to check in with both parties in a few days to see how things are going.

9. Thank the parties for coming together, and let them know that you are confident that they will be able to move forward on this situation.

Figure 2.2: Guiding staff members through conflict resolution.

Strategies for Staff Members to Use

Staff members need to learn how to stand up to others when being confronted. They can apply some of the same strategies that we have recommended for supervisors to use with Contrarians. For example, teaching staff members how to use content-reflecting and emotion-reflecting statements in situations with Contrarians can be a good investment in their own professional growth and also help them deal effectively with their colleagues. Consider using professional development time or staff meetings to help them learn and practice these new skills.

Summary

People who can look at all sides of an issue are important to the health and welfare of an organization. They serve an important function because they help a group see potential pitfalls and issues that could sidetrack an initiative. However, when their behavior becomes excessive or unceasing, they become Contrarians. Then they threaten the group by making you and others afraid to suggest ideas and strategies to keep the school on track for improvement. Contrarians also threaten to undermine your leadership and make others question your ideas. If a Contrarian gets away with confrontation designed just for the sake of argument, others may see this behavior as acceptable and adopt it themselves.

Contrarian behavior can spread on the staff and evolve into other negative and destructive behaviors. In order to prevent this scenario, you will need to act in a swift but purposeful manner. Keep in mind that when dealing with Contrarians, you must address their negative behaviors while avoiding unnecessary public confrontation. If their plight becomes public, they have the ability to turn key faculty members against you and make themselves martyrs. If this happens, staff sympathy will interfere with your efforts to remediate their behavior.

In this chapter you learned about techniques and strategies that will help you as you move forward in dealing with Contrarians on your staff. Not every idea suggested here will be appropriate for you or your school. Use the ones that best fit your needs and personality.

Questions for Reflection

Who are the Contrarians on your staff? What do you think caused their Contrarian behaviors to surface?

Why do Contrarians behave the way they do?

How does letting a Contrarian know that you are listening to him or her potentially lower the level of conflict?

What strategies and ideas do you think would best match your style and the culture of your school in dealing with a Contrarian?

How will you know when you are successful in remediating Contrarian behavior?

chapter 3

The Recruiters

Humans like to be a part of something. This drive is so strong that some people would rather get involved in something negative than not belong to anything at all. This basic need is what motivates the next group of difficult and resistant staff members we have to work with, the Recruiters.

As you read this chapter, you will learn the following:

- Typical behaviors of Recruiters and their impact on others

- Strategies for dealing with Recruiters

- The principal's role in creating Recruiters

- Ways to help develop the skills of other staff members to effectively deal with Recruiters

Behaviors and Impacts of Recruiters

Recruiters do not feel comfortable taking a stand on an issue alone. Thus they engage in the following behaviors:

- Cultivating relationships with staff members who are new or a little unsure of their place in the school community

- Constantly trying to win others over or get people to think like they do

- "Dropping" or sharing the names of others who agree with them or share their point of view

- Connecting with a variety of different groups based on the issue being discussed at the moment

These behaviors work together to have a potentially negative impact on individual staff members and the building as a whole. Here are some of the negative impacts we have seen over the years:

- The development of cliques or groups in a building—Recruiters are good at dividing staff members into factions or cliques. These alliances can be dangerous and work against the collaborative relationships you need to move your initiatives forward.

- An undermining of the confidence of some staff members—Recruiters can control the thoughts and opinions of some of the people they recruit. Those being controlled soon find that they have trouble making their own decisions or standing on their own two feet because of the influence the Recruiters have had over their opinions.

- An unrealistic perception of power—Once they are successful in their efforts to recruit others to their cause, Recruiters start to assume that they have power over or are the spokespeople for the rest of the staff members. This perception of power leads them to think that they are in charge and don't have to listen to you as the leader or to others on the faculty. This lack of accountability causes them to become outspoken and abrasive.

Let's see how one principal deals with a Recruiter who is working against her.

Scenario: They're All on My Side

Debbie, a high school principal, has a situation involving a strong Recruiter. As Debbie works with her staff to move forward on a project, she notices that Bill, one of her teachers, is talking with small groups of teachers on a regular basis. One evening after school, Bill organizes several other teachers and gets them to go to Debbie's office to share their concerns about the project. All of the teachers express the same concerns and refuse to move forward with the implementation. Debbie is surprised by the visit and the tone of the teachers. She thanks the teachers for coming to talk to her but reminds them of the process she has outlined for sharing and addressing staff concerns. She tells them that she will make note of their concerns but will need to talk to each of them individually if she is going to determine how she might provide the necessary resources to help them be successful with the new project. She sets follow-up appointments with each of the teachers to talk with them during the next week.

It is obvious that Bill recruited these teachers to confront Debbie and even told them what to say, since they mentioned the same concerns that Bill had expressed to her on an earlier occasion. She decides that she needs to talk to Bill and hold him accountable for his actions in recruiting the other teachers.

Lessons From This Scenario

There are many possible ways that Debbie could have handled this situation. A principal's selection of strategies will vary, depending on the unique culture of the school, the exact conditions of the situation, the principal's comfort level with different approaches, and so on. These are the steps we recommend:

- Be professional in your response to members of the "recruited group" when they ask to meet with you.

- Remind them that their behavior is not appropriate and that you can't solve their issues in this manner.

- Provide them with an alternative way to share their concerns.

- Allow them to move beyond the incident; let them know you still value your relationship with them and their professionalism.

- Arrange a meeting with the Recruiter. Plan to address the following points:

  - Remind the Recruiter of the process you have in place for resolving issues.

  - Find out his or her reasons for recruiting others.

  - Let the Recruiter know that even though he or she has the right to talk to others, it is not appropriate to stir them up or try to use a group to change your mind.

  - Remind the Recruiter of your expectations for communications and actions when he or she wants to resolve an issue in the future.

Further Strategies for Dealing With Recruiters

People with concerns sometimes band together because of their feeling that there is safety in numbers. They may have formed a group on their own, without the influence of a Recruiter. Before addressing a situation, think through it carefully and try to determine its foundation or origin. When you are convinced that you have identified a Recruiter on your staff, you face a delicate issue. On the one hand, you want to develop relationships and positive ways to solve problems, while on the other hand, you can't tell staff members that they can't talk to others about their concerns.

Here are some possible strategies to help you deal with Recruiters on your staff. The first strategies are more proactive and are intended to prevent recruiting situations from developing. The later strategies can be used when you become aware that recruiting is taking place.

- Head off Recruiters before they get started by developing a culture in which problems are resolved through planning and discussion. Hold open conversations with your faculty members about both positive situations and their concerns.

- Develop a step-by-step problem-solving process that you and your staff can follow. Recruiters can find fertile ground in cultures where there are underdeveloped problem-solving processes.

- When a staff member (especially one you think might have the potential to recruit others) has a concern, be sure to work hard to communicate to that person your interest in resolving the concern. Show him or her that you will do what it takes to listen and understand the problem.

- If you notice someone engaging in what looks like recruiting, schedule an appointment with that person, and check to see if you can help him or her with any issues.

- You may be able to use a Recruiter's strengths to influence the perceptions and behaviors of your staff in a positive way. If you work to help a Recruiter understand and support your project or initiative, he or she may be willing to help develop buy-in among the other staff members. This not only assists you in advancing your change effort but gives the Recruiter a positive outlet for his or her skills. It can be a win-win for both parties and for the school in general.

The Principal's Role in Creating Recruiters

Even though Recruiters can develop on their own or in response to other building situations, principals may have created conditions that allow Recruiters to thrive. In this section, we will look at some of the common ways principals do this and suggest the appropriate counterstrategies.

- Intimidating staff members and discouraging them from privately sharing their concerns—If principals do not listen with an open mind when staff members come to them with their concerns, they lay the seedbed for recruitment. Be sure that you truly listen to staff members when they come to you individually to express their concerns.

- Not having a formal process to resolve concerns—When staff members have no formalized vehicles to use to voice their concerns and have them addressed, they turn to Recruiters to fill this gap. Consider developing or adopting clear and specific procedures for staff members to use for sharing their concerns.

- Failing to recognize that staff members may not have the confidence or the strength to stand up on their own—Staff members need to learn and practice strategies that will enable them to clearly communicate their concerns in a positive and productive manner. You can help them build their skills in framing issues, asking for clarification, positively presenting their perspective, and using other essential advocacy strategies.

Working With Staff Members to Deal With Recruiters

All staff members need to be aware that recruiting others is a problem that can have negative implications for the school. Conduct sessions at staff meetings in which you discuss the damage that recruiting can cause. Then help the staff members find ways to work together to prevent Recruiters' behavior or deal with it when it occurs.

Group Norms

When faculty members develop their own operating norms, they tend to follow them. You can guide your staff in developing a norm against building coalitions or recruiting others to support certain positions related to implementation issues. A finished norm addressing recruiting might sound like this:

> As a faculty we agree that we need to respect diverse opinions in decision-making situations. We will not try to recruit others or develop coalitions to force opinions or ideas on others. Our decision-making process will use consensus rather than voting or other power techniques.

If the staff members do not have the skills or confidence to develop a norm, you may want to develop a ground rule that prohibits recruiting. A ground rule is set by the leader to control behavior from outside of the group. It provides for faster problem resolution but does not allow for the group's investment in solving the problem. A ground rule might be phrased as follows:

> No one on the faculty will try to recruit others to support his or her side of an issue. Discussions of issues will occur in the open and allow individuals to share their unique perspectives before we make a collaborative decision.

Once a group norm or ground rule has been established, it will be your job to follow up and make sure that the group adheres to it.

Problem-Solving Process

It is essential for the leader to develop a clear problem-solving and complaint-resolution process. Put it in writing, and teach everyone on the staff how to use it for communicating concerns. Provide this training at professional development sessions and faculty meetings. Here is an example of a process you might consider adopting:

1   If you have a concern, let the person causing this concern know that you'd like to talk with him or her.

2   If the concern cannot be resolved at this level, notify your administrator about the issue. Ask her to mediate a conversation between you and the person you are in conflict with.

3   If the conflict or concern cannot be resolved at this mediation, ask the administrator to make a decision based on the facts presented during the mediation session. Both parties will need to abide by the decision made by the administrator.

Building Staff Members' Skills

- When confronted by a Recruiter and a team of recruits, explain to them that a show of numbers is not the best way to influence your decisions or change your mind on an issue. Remind the group of the processes that have been established for identifying and resolving problems, and redirect them back through those processes.

- Help staff members recognize the manipulation techniques Recruiters are attempting to use. Help them keep their guard up.

- Assess those most vulnerable to recruitment; build them up so they feel confident standing on their own versus being manipulated by the Recruiter. Teach them how to hold on to their own opinion and not be influenced so easily by others.

- Let staff members know the importance of collaboration and team development. Help them build up their own leadership skills so that they can channel Recruiters' energy toward positive efforts in the school.

"Ripple Effects" Activity

In our work with school leaders and school improvement teams, one of the most beneficial activities we have introduced is called "Ripple Effects."

The idea is to look at the proposed project or school improvement plan and analyze it for potential unforeseen or unintended effects. Without this type of process, leaders and school improvement teams are often surprised and overtaken by events they did not anticipate.

We are including the activity here because in many cases, failing to plan for these ripple effects can facilitate or reinforce difficult and resistant behaviors such as recruiting. If you can think through the potential problems in a plan or project, you can lower the chance your project will encounter unforeseen negative impacts.

This activity is designed to be completed by a team or group that is responsible for implementing a change or is directly impacted by a change. We have used it with groups ranging from administrative teams to whole faculty groups.

The activity works like this:

1   Each group member is given four to five sticky notes.

2   The new idea, program, or change that is being considered for implementation is written on a large sheet of chart paper in the center of a diagram that follows the template in figure 3.1. Individuals are given two to three minutes to think of as many potential ripple effects or impacts of the implementation as they can. They write each one on a separate sticky note.

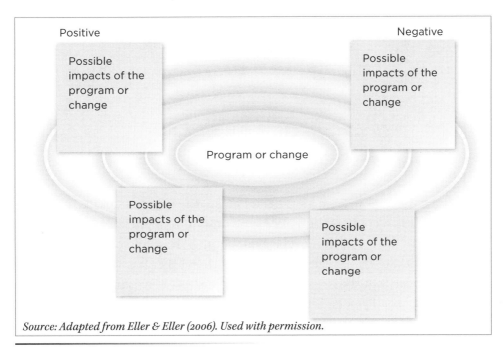

Source: Adapted from Eller & Eller (2006). Used with permission.

Figure 3.1: "Ripple Effects" template.

3   Once the thinking time has expired, team members are asked to come up to the chart and place their sticky notes on the pond ripples whose distance from the center corresponds to approximately when these impacts could occur in the school. For example, impacts that might occur soon after the idea is implemented are placed closer to the center, while those that might occur later are placed on the outer parts of the diagram. Duplicate sticky notes will not necessarily end up in the same position—it is up to the individual team member to determine where his or her note belongs. Sticky notes containing positive impacts should be placed on the left side of the chart, and those with negative impacts should be placed on the right side of the chart. Figure 3.2 shows a sample diagram that has been completed.

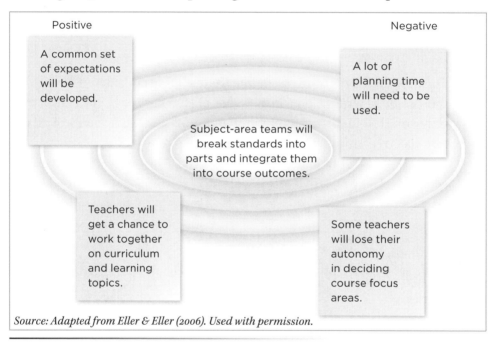

Source: Adapted from Eller & Eller (2006). Used with permission.

Figure 3.2: Completed "Ripple Effects" diagram.

4   Once the sticky notes have been placed, the group members should engage in a conversation about the potential impacts of the idea or project. The group can make a list of the potentially positive and negative ripple effects. The group should then talk about the strategies or resources that the organization may possess or acquire to minimize the potentially negative ripple effects.

This activity helps a group visualize a project or an idea and anticipate some of the pitfalls that could come with it. By identifying potential pitfalls up front, you and your team can work to minimize or eliminate them before they become issues. And without major issues to complain about, difficult or resistant people can have a harder time gaining an audience or recruiting a support group that could undermine your initiative.

Summary

Recruiters try to find people they can get on their side to build coalitions and support for their way of thinking. Because they generally focus on the negative aspects of school improvement projects, their behaviors can undermine your work as a leader. Left unchecked, they can cause major issues within the school and hinder your efforts to improve school climate and culture. You should find ways to diminish their influence over your staff. Watching out for Recruiters and dealing with them as early as possible can help you keep your projects positive and on track. As is the case when handling other types of difficult and resistant staff members, addressing Recruiters' behaviors requires you to think through the issues and develop a game plan that will fit the situation, your comfort as the principal, and the culture of the school.

Questions for Reflection

Who are the Recruiters on your staff? How might you go about figuring out who they are?

What might you do to decrease the chances that Recruiters will emerge or develop in your school?

If they are left unchecked, what damage can Recruiters do to your improvement initiatives and the climate and culture of your school?

Why do people engage in recruiting others to support their ideas or opinions? How can you minimize the impact of Recruiters in your school?

What are some ways you could address a Recruiter in your building?

chapter 4

The Challenged

Sometimes people become difficult or resistant to cover up the fact that they cannot perform the task or assignment being asked of them in the change effort. We can all control our resistance but not our capabilities, so this can be an easy route to take. People who are incapable and try to cover it up are dangerous to the school climate and culture. We call these people "the Challenged."

As you read this chapter, you will learn the following:

- Typical behaviors of the Challenged
- How to diagnose an employee's level of competence
- Ways to help the Challenged to be more successful
- The principal's role in creating the Challenged
- Ways to respectfully involve other staff members in helping the Challenged grow and learn

Behaviors of the Challenged

Challenged staff members do not want to be pushed to perform tasks or learn skills that fall outside of their comfort zone or their current frame of reference. They may have developed this resistance because of a fear of failure or because they have never received the necessary support to learn and implement the skills required to do a good job in a new assignment. As we stress throughout this book, it is important to try to understand what may be causing a staff member to be difficult or resistant before you take steps to address the problematic behavior.

Challenged staff members typically act in the following ways:

- They are convinced they are doing well with their existing practice and justify their old behaviors.

- They cover up their lack of knowledge by discounting new ideas or strategies.

- They keep doing the same things, even if they don't work. When the old methods don't work, they blame students, parents, or others.

Let's look at a situation in which a principal finds himself dealing with a Challenged staff member.

Scenario: They Just Can't Learn

Juan, the principal of an elementary school, has one teacher on his staff whose teaching style constantly draws complaints from parents and other staff members. This teacher, Fanny, has not implemented any of the strategies for increasing student engagement that were the focus of this year's staff development program. When Juan brings up this point to Fanny, she normally changes the subject, avoids the issue, and tells Juan that her students' lack of skills prevents her from effectively implementing the new strategies.

Juan decides to have an honest conversation with Fanny about the situation. He begins by saying, "Fanny, I want to have an open and off-the-record conversation with you about your implementation of the new initiative here in the building. I know you are on evaluation cycle this year, but this conversation will not be a part of the normal evaluation process." After this reassurance, he goes on to say, "I want to help you. Please tell me what is keeping you from using the strategies we talked about in our professional development session that we held last fall." Fanny hesitates and gives Juan the normal excuses but finally admits that she just does not understand how to use these strategies in her classroom.

Juan thanks Fanny for being honest with him and then tells her, "I will help you learn and use these ideas in your classroom. As long as you are sincere in your efforts to learn and keep trying to implement the strategies in your classroom, our work will not be a part of the teacher evaluation process." Then, together, they establish a learning plan through which Fanny will get the help she needs to be successful. Juan also creates a follow-up plan to make visits to her classroom to see how things are going. Fanny is still a little tentative about implementing the new skills but has taken the first step to learn and grow.

Lessons From This Scenario

In this case, Juan was able to get Fanny to admit her deficiencies. He then met her where she was in relation to the skills needed to successfully implement the new ideas and helped her develop a plan to learn and move forward in a step-by-step manner. In many cases involving Challenged staff members, however, you are going to have to figure out for yourself that the person is incapable of implementing the new strategy and then develop the learning and follow-up plans.

Here are some other approaches that might be used in addressing a situation such as the one Juan encountered with Fanny:

- Observe in the Challenged teacher's classroom using a random schedule. Watch for deficiencies in her performance relative to the needs for the new idea or innovation. Design a growth plan for her to begin to address these needs.

- Meet with the teacher and tell her specifically what she needs to improve on in her teaching. Offer the services of an instructional coach to help her learn the new skills and behaviors she needs in order to be successful. Meet with her and the instructional coach to outline the services that will be offered to her and when they will be delivered. Develop a plan that includes follow-up strategies to check in and see how things are going.

- Meet with the teacher to address her attitude toward the skills required for the implementation of the new ideas. Let her know that you understand that she is unsure of exactly how to implement these new ideas and that you plan to work with her. Tell her that you will try to help her informally and outside of the normal teacher evaluation system to give her a chance to learn the skills now expected of her. Working informally to help the teacher learn a new skill rather than evaluating her performance can help her be more receptive to learning and less concerned that she is being judged. It also removes some of the positional power that can be present in typical evaluation relationships. Informal help can come in the form of coaching and working in collaboration with the teacher. In exchange for this arrangement, you should communicate your expectation that she will remain positive about the new ideas at staff meetings and in talking with other colleagues.

Further Strategies for Working With the Challenged

Challenged people pose a complex problem for school improvement initiatives because they can be hard to discover, and once you find them, they may deny that they are having trouble carrying out the requirements of the innovation you are implementing. Some Challenged staff members do a good job of covering up their deficiencies and pretending that they know what is going on. It may take a variety of strategies to help them learn what they need to be successful and less difficult and negative. Here are some ideas:

- If you are going to help staff members learn the skills they need to implement a new initiative, you first have to be clear yourself about what skills the initiative requires. Use the "Skill Analysis Template" (fig. 4.1) to list the specific skills and to break them down into sub-skills. Visit **go.solution-tree.com/leadership** to download this and other tools in this chapter.

Skill Analysis Template

Learning a new skill, strategy, or behavior can be a difficult experience. Use this template to assist you in identifying the new skills your initiative requires. Then break the skills down into parts that can make implementation easier and more of a step-by-step process for your staff members.

1. What is the general goal or outcome of the initiative or project?

2. What are the specific skills, strategies, or behaviors that staff members will need to use in order to successfully reach the general goal or outcome? List them in the order in which they will need to be learned.

    Specific skill 1:

    Specific skill 2:

    Specific skill 3:

    Specific skill 4:

    Specific skill 5:

    Specific skill 6:

    Specific skill 7:

3. Break each skill down into the subskills that staff members will need to learn in order to master it.

    Specific skill 1
        Subskill:

        Subskill:

        Subskill:

Specific skill 2
    Subskill:

    Subskill:

    Subskill:

Specific skill 3
    Subskill:

    Subskill:

    Subskill:

Specific skill 4
    Subskill:

    Subskill:

    Subskill:

Specific skill 5
    Subskill:

    Subskill:

    Subskill:

Specific skill 6
    Subskill:

    Subskill:

    Subskill:

Specific skill 7
    Subskill:

    Subskill:

    Subskill:

Figure 4.1: Identifying the skills a new initiative requires.

- Provide multiple opportunities for staff members to learn about the details and strategies associated with the new initiatives.

- Check in with staff members individually to make sure they understand the new program and what is expected from them. Ask them questions that will verify their understanding. If you discover gaps in their learning, make note of them, and provide resources to help the staff members be successful.

- In the initial stages of the new program, ask teachers to invite you to lessons in which they are trying out or using the new skills they have learned in their professional development sessions. You will quickly see who knows what to do and who is struggling to learn the new expectations. Reinforce those who are on track, and provide coaching and feedback to those who are still learning or need additional assistance.

- When you feel a person has questions or is unable to understand an essential component of the new program, schedule an informal meeting with him or her to talk about it. Offer additional support yourself or through coaching to help individual staff members learn what they need in order to be successful.

- When a person is struggling with the implementation, carefully think through exactly what he or she needs to be successful. Identify the skills the person needs with the "Missing Skills Identification Template" (fig. 4.2), and help him or her break the skills down into parts using the "Skill Analysis Template" (fig. 4.1, pages 46–47).

- Develop a growth plan with clear objectives and timelines to help the person learn the new skills. Use the scheduling component at the bottom of the "Missing Skills Identification Template."

The Principal's Role in Creating the Challenged

Principals and schools sometimes inadvertently create Challenged staff members. In this section, we will look at some of the common ways this happens and suggest the appropriate counterstrategies.

- Fails to clearly communicate teaching expectations to staff members—Many principals do not possess the skills or feel they have the time to talk about their expectations regarding the use of effective instructional strategies. The best time to communicate these expectations is at regularly or specially scheduled staff meetings in which instructional strategies are the topic of discussion.

- Not providing adequate support in past initiatives—If staff members did not get good professional development, follow-up coaching, and other types of follow-up support, they may not have learned the essentials to be successful in using new strategies. When you implement new programs and initiatives, be sure to build in adequate learning opportunities for your staff.

Missing Skills Identification Template

Staff member:

Subject area:

1. Clear description of missing skills needed to successfully implement the new initiative:

2. Rank-ordering of skills needed (list foundational or most crucial skills first, followed by other skills in the order needed):

3. Schedule of when new skills will be introduced and when you hope the staff member will be able to use the new skills in the classroom (write down the months when the new skills will be introduced and reinforced):

Skill	Month	Introduce (I) or Reinforce (R)

Figure 4.2: Identifying the skills an employee needs to develop.

- Not supporting risk taking or trying out new ideas—In some schools, the culture reinforces the status quo and squelches innovation and risk taking. In these cultures, staff members actually tell colleagues not to try new things or give them a hard time when they "go out on a limb." The consequences for attempting new approaches and failing are greater than those for maintaining ineffective behaviors. Be sure to assess your culture to figure out its receptiveness to innovation and risk taking. Encourage staff members to try new ideas, and reinforce their efforts when they do.

- Punishing or scolding teachers when they try new ideas and fail—If teachers who initially fail when they try new ideas are reprimanded or suddenly put on the evaluation cycle, they quickly learn not to try new strategies. Be careful with the feedback you provide to staff members when they are trying new ideas. Offer to let them try their new strategies informally or outside of the normal staff evaluation process. These approaches let people know that you support them during the trial-and-error phase of a new initiative.

Working With Staff Members to Help the Challenged

Engaging other staff members in helping those who need support and development to better implement new ideas can be somewhat tricky. One of the reasons the Challenged become difficult and resistant is that they *don't* want others to know that they need assistance. Keeping that in mind, here are some strategies that you can consider for working with other staff members to increase the competencies of the Challenged:

- Provide a "picture" or vision of where the new initiative or project is going and what you intend for the staff and students to learn and be able to do by the end of the first semester and first year. Describing how things will look gives staff members another opportunity to understand what's expected of them. The visual description will also serve you and your school well when it comes time to assess the success of the project. Table 4.1 can be used to develop a specific vision.

- Hold informational meetings with all staff members to help them understand and discuss the important attributes of the new program.

- Hold optional sharing sessions, open to all staff members, in which teachers can bring and share examples of their implementation, including lesson plans, assessment documents, student work, and so on.

- Conduct optional problem-solving meetings with staff members in which teachers come together around common issues and questions. Small groups can be put together on an impromptu basis to talk about common concerns.

- Use peer coaches and mentors to help people get support as they are learning new skills and ideas.

Table 4.1: Project Visioning Chart

Project Name:			
At the end of the semester, what will we be able to see happening in our classrooms if we are successful in implementing this project?		At the end of the year, what will we be able to see happening in our classrooms if we are successful in implementing this project?	
Student Learning	**Teaching Methods**	**Student Learning**	**Teaching Methods**

Summary

They may seem innocent enough, but staff members who do not have the skills to implement strategies related to a new initiative can be difficult and resistant. As their leader, you want to be able to look beyond their avoidance behaviors and determine exactly what support they need in order to be successful.

In this chapter, we have shared ideas and strategies for you to use in working with the Challenged on your staff. The stakes for their improvement are high because what they do directly affects their students' achievement and self-concepts. Challenged staff members also have an impact on the success of the rest of the school. In our era of accountability, it is easy for everyone to see when the Challenged teachers' students fall behind. The other teachers may wonder why you are not doing anything about the Challenged teachers' deficient teaching skills and may resent the fact that they have to work harder with their students to make up for the learning deficits caused by their Challenged colleagues. On a more hopeful note, among all the types of difficult and resistant staff members that we discuss in this book, the Challenged are the group on whom you can make the greatest impact with patient and focused improvement efforts.

Questions for Reflection

Who are the Challenged in your school? How might you go about identifying them?

Why do the Challenged pose a threat to your school climate and culture?

When the Challenged don't do what they are supposed to do, how can you determine whether it is because of a lack of ability (as opposed to stubbornness)?

How can you break down the skills your Challenged staff members need? How can you begin to develop the Challenged into more competent teachers?

What are some resources you can provide to Challenged staff members to help them improve their performance?

chapter 5

The On-the-Job Retirees

Believe it or not, there are some staff members whose major desire is to be left alone and allowed to coast until they are eligible for retirement. We call these people the "On-the-Job Retirees." Everywhere we have served as principals, we have encountered people wanting to retire on the job. These staff members hold the potential to pull down the rest of the faculty and can also cause you extra work because you might have to deal with students and parents who complain to you about these teachers' sometimes poor performance.

As you read this chapter, you will learn the following:

- Traits and behaviors of On-the-Job Retirees
- Strategies for working with On-the-Job Retirees
- The principal's role in creating On-the-Job Retirees
- Ways to help develop the skills of other staff members to effectively deal with On-the-Job Retirees in their midst

Traits and Behaviors of On-the-Job Retirees

Here are some traits and behaviors that are commonly associated with On-the-Job Retirees:

- A lack of motivation beyond getting by day to day
- A diminished work ethic
- Lack of interest in contributing to the overall success of the school
- Being openly verbal about their upcoming retirement and their desire to coast their way out of the job

- Watching the clock; arriving at the last possible minute and leaving as soon as possible after the work day has ended

On-the-Job Retirees can cause all kinds of problems because of their lack of commitment and their disregard for policy and procedures. As school leaders, we need to be able to recognize their behaviors and address them quickly and completely.

Let's see how one principal responds to a teacher who is operating in retirement mode.

Scenario: Leave Me Alone, I'm in Retirement Mode

Jerry, the principal of Oceanside Elementary School, and the other members of the leadership team want to implement professional learning communities (PLCs) in their building. They decide that they will make PLCs a professional goal in their school improvement plan. Over the summer, the leadership team receives training on PLCs. At their first staff meeting in the fall, the members of the leadership team present the school improvement plan to the staff and explain how PLCs will be implemented at their school. As in many schools when something is new, there are many questions about how this will affect the school and, most important, how it will affect the staff members personally. Many staff members are excited about having the opportunity to work as a team rather than in isolation. Of course, there are some staff members who think PLCs are a new idea that will quickly fade, like so many other things in education.

The following day, the leadership team meets to discuss the next step in getting PLCs started. During the meeting, Mary, one of the team members, mentions that she has received an email from a colleague named Don, who basically said that he wasn't going to participate in the PLC group because he was in retirement mode. He also told her that he wasn't about to work with some of his colleagues. The team members discuss how to work with employees who are resistant to change. They feel it is important to have some training on how to deal with resistant employees.

Jerry thinks it would be best if he met with Don. He sends Don an email asking to meet with him to discuss PLCs. At their meeting, Don announces, "I'm not planning to participate in a PLC, because I'm going to retire at the end of the year, and I don't need to get involved in anything new." Jerry replies that, as far as he is concerned, Don needs to give 100 percent every day at Oceanside ES and that he is expected to be a part of the PLC.

This makes Don bristle. He says, "I have always given 110 percent at my job. I have been a valuable member of this staff for thirty-six years, and I don't like that you are questioning my loyalty and motives."

Picking up on Don's justifiable pride in the impact he has had on the staff and the school, Jerry tells him, "You have contributed so much here over the years; I want people to remember you as the leader you have worked hard to become." He goes on to say that Don has a lot of knowledge and talent to offer the PLC group and that he is an important part of the team. Then he asks him, "Will you give 100 percent in your classroom and at the PLC meetings?"

Don replies, "I'm tired, but I want others to see me as a leader. I'll give it my best shot."

After the meeting, Jerry writes a memo to Don, recapping what they discussed. Jerry then makes sure to touch base with Mary because she is the leader of Don's PLC. He tells her that it would be good to get Don involved at the first meeting and suggests that she ask Don to share a teaching strategy that has been effective with his students. As the principal at Oceanside, Jerry knows it is important to have Don feel he is a valuable part of the PLC. Having Don share a teaching strategy with the PLC team will hold Don accountable to the team. It will also send a message to the team that everyone will be a part of the process of change.

After the first PLC meeting, many staff members tell Jerry that Don has been using the retirement excuse for many years. Some staff members tell him that they are glad to see that Don is being held accountable.

Jerry will continue to check in with Don to see how things are going in the PLC group.

Lessons From This Scenario

In this particular scenario, we saw that Don thought he would get away with his resistant behavior and be allowed to just sit back and do whatever he wanted until he retired. Jerry knew that the other staff members were watching how he handled Don and would base their opinion of him on how he dealt with the situation.

When working with On-the-Job Retirees, you have to maintain a respectful and professional relationship while being careful not to set the stage for an age-discrimination allegation. Since this book is not designed to provide specific legal advice for you and your state, be sure to seek legal advice if you have any reservations about moving forward with an employee.

There are a number of ways that you can be respectful yet firm. We saw Jerry use several of the following strategies with Don:

- Appeal to the employee's professionalism. Don had served the school and district well in the past. Jerry appealed to Don's previous dedication and past service as a way to help keep him on track. A principal can make comments like "I know you have a legacy here. You don't want to go out leaving people with the impression that you are not dedicated." Such comments make a clear connection between an employee and his or her accomplishments. They not only reinforce the person for past work but set a standard for the future.

- Be clear in letting the employee know your expectations for his or her performance and involvement in the school's programs. Sharing clear and focused expectations can go a long way toward keeping the employee on track. As we saw with the way that Jerry handled Don, you will need to be assertive and frank. You could make statements like "I know you only have seven months left here, but during that time I expect that you will fully participate in all school programs" or "I know you are thinking about what you will do after retirement, but during your time here I want to make sure you know exactly what I expect from you." It is essential to be clear but respectful as you talk with your On-the-Job Retirees to maintain their dignity while helping them stay focused.

- Offer to help or provide extra guidance. Many people who are at a more advanced career stage may benefit from additional guidance from you as their supervisor. Spending more time in their classrooms, coaching them, or even co-teaching with them may provide some external motivation or support. Conversely, some teachers might be motivated to stay focused on their job in order to keep you out of their classrooms! In either case, the offer of providing extra help may be just what someone like Don needs to keep him active and engaged throughout his remaining days on the staff.

- Consider allowing the employee to start implementing a part of the new program or initiative. At times, your most experienced staff members may find new initiatives or programs challenging to think about. Allowing someone like Don to get involved with a part of the new initiative and doing it really well may help him concentrate and implement the new idea one step at a time while saving face with you and his other colleagues.

- Set up a follow-up plan. We saw that Jerry intended to follow up with Don. This would let Don know that Jerry was watching him and was invested in his success. A follow-up plan does not necessarily need to be a part of the performance evaluation system but can be personalized to meet the employee's unique needs. We will discuss follow-up in more detail in chapter 9.

Further Strategies for Working With On-the-Job Retirees

Letting On-the-Job Retirees just do whatever they want is a mistake and something that may come back to haunt you. It's important to respond both quickly and professionally when you encounter someone who thinks he or she can just coast through the school year. Here are some more ideas we have found to be beneficial when working with On-the-Job Retirees:

- When you hear that an employee has declared him- or herself "retired" before the end of the year, respond quickly to meet with that employee.

- Use peer pressure.

- Put the employee on the formal evaluation cycle.

- Conduct a private meeting with the employee to talk about his or her intentions and plans for the future.

- Work with the employee to develop a private succession plan to help him or her stay focused and on track.

- Provide the employee with an important task or job that will utilize his or her skills as a professional.

- Develop a growth plan to make sure the employee stays on track.

- Get the employee's retirement or resignation in writing; make sure the board acts on it right away.

- Offer a trade-off: the employee's continued engagement for a reduction of some other responsibility.

- Conduct the "What Will Be Your Legacy?" activity. This exercise, which is shown in figure 5.1 (page 58), asks participants to contemplate what they want their legacy at the school to be once they leave the job. It is a powerful activity because it allows the person considering retirement to think about his or her potential impact on others. Many people at this stage just "drift away" from the profession. You provide a real gift to those who will be retiring by asking them to consider the legacy they want to leave. Visit **go.solution-tree.com/ leadership** to download this exercise.

What Will Be Your Legacy?

As you think about leaving the profession, it is important that you consider what you will leave behind to help your peers and the profession. This worksheet will assist you in developing your legacy. Please respond to the following questions:

1. What have you learned or gained over your years in the profession?

2. Project yourself into the future one year after your retirement. What is it that you think you have positively influenced, contributed to, or transformed as a result of your work in the building? What would not be the same or as positive here if it weren't for you and your efforts or influence?

3. It's now five years since you've retired. What positive comments are current staff members who worked with you saying about your time here? How have you changed or influenced their lives? How are things different here as a result of the time you spent at the building?

4. Putting together all that you have reflected on in this exercise, what is the legacy that you want to leave here and have others remember you by after you leave?

Figure 5.1: An activity for staff members nearing retirement.

The Principal's Role in Creating On-the-Job Retirees

Principals can unknowingly create On-the-Job Retirees with their comments and actions. In this section, we will look at some of the common ways this happens and suggest the appropriate counterstrategies.

- Giving older staff employees less attention and responsibility— The teachers' natural response to this treatment is to pull away from the school and their colleagues. Such alienation can accelerate the development of On-the-Job Retirees. Savvy principals know how to engage aging staff members in school improvement strategies and new initiatives. You can keep senior staff members connected by recognizing and valuing the unique perspective that they bring to the school.

- Taking the opposite approach and giving experienced teachers an unfair burden of responsibility in the school—Senior teachers might be assigned more strenuous duties, harder students and parents, and more preparations. This will drain their energy and hurt their attitude. Watch how you distribute duties and difficult situations among the staff to ensure that everyone is doing his or her fair share to help the school be successful.

- Giving more credibility to newer staff members—In schools, it is attractive to work with new teachers. They bring fresh energy and enthusiasm to the job. You should look at all staff members and identify their unique contributions to the school community. This process will allow the blending of strengths and experiences rather than the segregation of staff members.

- In an attempt to remain collegial, giving On-the-Job Retirees the impression that they accept their behavior—Senior staff members may joke about the fact that they are contemplating retirement or cutting back on their work. Be careful about agreeing with them. Reinforcing their message over time may accelerate their disconnection from the school. Instead, try to keep them focused on their strengths and positive contributions to the school and the rest of the faculty.

Working With Staff Members to Keep On-the-Job Retirees Engaged

It is important for you to help your staff members understand the different age groups represented in the building and the strengths each group brings to the workplace. This is a worthwhile topic to discuss at a staff meeting. A good way to approach this topic is to introduce an activity called "Generations." The exercise will help your staff begin to understand how members from different age groups think. Here are the steps to follow in conducting this activity:

1 Before the activity, identify the major eras of birth that represent the faculty (for example, identify the numbers of people born in the 1950s, 1960s, 1970s, and so on).

2 Take a large sheet of chart paper for each of the birth eras identified. On each sheet, write the era and the following questions:

- What were the most popular movies that came out while you were in high school?

- What were the most popular books on the market while you were in high school?

- What were people's ideas and values related to their work when you first started in the profession? How has that changed or evolved over the years?

3 Position the charts in a circle around the room. Ask all of the staff members to gather by the chart that corresponds to the era in which they were born.

4 Have each group respond to the prompts on its respective chart.

5 Next, the entire faculty will learn about the experiences and beliefs of each era by following these steps:

- The staff members at each chart will select one member to stay at the chart to explain what the group generated.

- The other members will travel to other charts to learn what the rest of the groups generated.

- Each traveler group rotates clockwise from one chart to the next, staying for three to four minutes at each chart to listen to the presentation from the designated spokesperson. The groups can rotate to music, as in the game musical chairs.

- The traveler group members continue to rotate until they return to the chart of their own era.

6 Once back at their own charts, the group members talk about what they learned about the perspectives of the representatives of the other eras.

7 Reconvene the large group, and ask the faculty members to talk about what they learned about one another as a result of the activity and how they can use this information to work together and support one another.

Another powerful strategy for helping staff members deal with On-the-Job Retirees is to set up mentorships. These arrangements can be handled in two ways: you can invite staff members to connect with and act as informal mentors to On-the-Job Retirees, or you can ask On-the-Job-Retirees to mentor younger, less-experienced staff members with your guidance.

Summary

On-the-Job Retirees can be challenging staff members to work with. In some cases, they think they don't have anything to lose, so they can do whatever they want. If you recognize their coasting behavior and confront it, you can turn them around and keep all of your employees motivated and on track.

On-the-Job Retirees have the potential not only to lose their own sense of worth and value to the organization but also to affect the attitudes of others on your staff. When other teachers see them getting away with their efforts to resist change, they may start to think that they don't need to adopt new ideas. The lowering of self-expectations will eventually have a negative impact on your school's climate and culture.

In this chapter, we have provided ideas and strategies to help you identify On-the-Job Retirees and begin to impact their disconnected behaviors. You may think that a proper strategy is just to wait them out and let them retire in grace. In the long run, however, not addressing their behaviors does more damage than good. It lowers your credibility as a leader and sets the stage for future dissent from others on your staff. We hope the strategies you have learned in this chapter will enable you to take the bull by the horns and work with your senior staff members to keep them engaged and productive until they actually do retire.

Questions for Reflection

What are some of the characteristics of On-the-Job Retirees?

How can you begin to alter the behavior of these employees by immediately meeting with them and confronting the situation?

What situations and behaviors may contribute to a senior staff member's lack of connection and engagement?

Who on your staff holds the potential to become an On-the-Job Retiree? How might you intervene with those people before their behaviors get out of control?

How can identifying the legacy an employee might leave at a school help keep a potential On-the-Job Retiree on track?

chapter 6

The Resident Experts

Everyone has dealt with people who seem to have knowledge about almost every topic and want to share their opinions without even being asked to share them. We call these people the "Resident Experts." When you talk with them about the new initiative, they assure you that they know exactly what to do and how to implement the essential elements, but when you observe them in action, they are doing things incorrectly. As you try to clarify what needs to be done differently, you get the response, "I know what to do." In your heart, you know that this person does not know what to do but is trying to save face by telling you he or she does.

As you read this chapter, you will learn the following:

- Typical behaviors of Resident Experts
- Strategies for handling Resident Experts
- The principal's role in creating Resident Experts
- Ways to help develop the skills of other staff members to effectively deal with Resident Experts in their midst

Behaviors of Resident Experts

These staff members always seem to know everything about every topic. No matter what you tell them, they know better and don't plan to listen to your ideas. They cause difficulty in schools because they will eventually run into trouble and mess up what they are implementing. Here are some typical behaviors that Resident Experts exhibit:

- They make it clear that they know everything about the new initiative, and they are not shy about sharing with their peers.

- They tune out or fail to listen to key information or directions related to the new initiative or program because they believe they already know all there is to know about it.

- They spend energy covering up the fact that they don't really know what to do.

- When they do not implement strategies correctly, they do not take responsibility for the situation. They contend that some outside force has caused the problem.

- They pretend they know what you are talking about and cut you off partway through your presentation, or they appear to be listening but are not focused on what you are saying.

- They avoid having you observe them trying out or implementing the new initiative, or they keep finding excuses for why they have not yet started the implementation.

- Even though they can't implement the new strategies, they make others on your staff feel inadequate about their own skills.

Scenario: I Know Better

Kathy, the principal of a middle school, is reviewing some of the files for her special education programs when she notices something different about the assessment information that Darrell, one of her special education teachers, has submitted. His annual reviews of the students on his caseload do not contain any local assessment data. To comply with the district's response to intervention (RTI) program, all of the teachers have been required to gather periodic assessment information to use in making student programming decisions. It appears that Darrell is either not gathering this information or not including it in his student reports. Kathy knows that Darrell's omission of this crucial information raises compliance issues and could put the program and the entire district in jeopardy of losing special education funding, so she decides to meet with him and confront him about the situation.

Kathy sets up an after-school meeting with Darrell. She has copies of his student progress reports and opens the meeting by asking him to explain his student assessment process. Darrell says, "I use a variety of sources when making my determination of student progress."

Since Kathy thinks he is avoiding the issue, she asks him directly, "Are you using the RTI process and the forms the district has provided in your assessment system?" At first, Darrell tries to sidestep the issue but then admits that he has not been using the required process and forms.

Kathy says, "Tell me why you have not been using the required process in assessing your students."

Darrell replies, "Kathy, I've been assessing students for twenty years, and I know how to do it. This new RTI process is just a fad that will quickly fade away. I always get accurate results with my methods."

Kathy is upset but keeps calm and says, "We have to follow the district policy on student assessment. We can't submit this paperwork and expect to be in compliance with the new regulations. You must use the RTI process for assessing your students and reporting their progress."

Darrell tries to argue his point, but Kathy will not back down. She says to Darrell, "I know you may have your own opinion on this, but I am directing you to use the new RTI process in assessing your students. I will be happy to provide you with the support you need in order to learn how to use this process in your classroom." Then Kathy sets up a schedule for Darrell to learn and practice using the RTI process for his student assessments. She also tells him that she wants to schedule an observation in the next week to watch him using the RTI skills he is learning. Finally, Kathy tells Darrell that if he does not use the RTI process in his classroom, she will need to meet with him again and consider more serious disciplinary action. Darrell gets the message from Kathy that this is a serious issue and that she will be checking to make sure he is in compliance with district policy.

Lessons From This Scenario

Kathy used her positional power as the principal to get Darrell to comply with district policy and use RTI strategies for assessment. She issued him a directive and followed through with a warning of consequences if he did not abide by it. Here are some other strategies she might use in this situation:

- Kathy could get Darrell's classroom covered and meet with him during school hours to discuss the problem. In this meeting she could find out why he was not implementing the RTI process and take action based on his response. If she thought that he needed time to learn the process, she could provide him with a substitute to cover his class while he learned. She could then follow up to make sure that he was using the required process.

- If Kathy thought that Darrell needed additional motivation to implement RTI strategies, she could ask him to meet with her and the district special education director. The presence of a higher-level administrator helps a teacher understand the severity of an issue.

- Once Kathy had given Darrell the directive to start using RTI, she could require him to file weekly reports containing the charts and other information that he used in assessing his students. Kathy and Darrell could meet each week, and he could outline what he had done in relation to the RTI process in his classroom.

- If Kathy felt that Darrell needed additional learning support to implement the RTI process, she could assign him to work with the department chair or another teacher. She could meet with Darrell and the other teacher periodically to talk about his progress.

Further Strategies for Handling Resident Experts

Because Resident Experts do not like to be given instructions or advice, you need to figure out how to communicate with them in a way that will demand their attention. We recommend the following strategies.

- Assume nothing; break down information into small, easy-to-understand parts. As you explain processes and procedures, take time to cover all of the details. Resident experts may interrupt you and tell you that they know what to do. You need to insist that they listen to the entire explanation before interrupting you. This insistence will sound like the framing statements we describe in chapter 2. Here are some examples:

    - "I know this may seem like a repeat of what you already know, but I want you to listen through my entire idea before interjecting any of your thoughts."

    - "As I describe the new initiative to you, you need to resist the temptation to interject your own ideas or put your unique spin on it."

    - "I know it can be hard for you to listen to something you think you already know a lot about, but please let me finish my description before you jump in with your thoughts."

    - "You may think that you already know this, but I have a new twist on the situation that you need to listen carefully to. After I finish, I will ask for your thoughts."

Use the following process for providing directions to Resident Experts:

1   Once you have determined that the Resident Expert does not have all of the details or does not know what to do in relation to your project or

initiative, perform an analysis of the steps or tasks needed to successfully implement it (see fig. 4.1, pages 46–47, for an analysis process).

2   Write out a list of the specific steps or have them in mind as you begin talking to the Resident Expert about what he or she needs to do. Be ready to share these details in a step-by-step manner.

3   Use a framing statement to start the conversation and keep the Resident Expert from getting off track. Be ready to use framing statements throughout the conversation whenever the Resident Expert gets off track.

It is important to develop your nonverbal communication techniques as well. Pairing certain gestures with your framing statements works even better than just telling people that the conversation must stay on track. The gestures described in table 6.1 will add more authority and power to your delivery. We perform a gesture right after making a framing statement to reinforce the verbal message. When dealing with extremely difficult or resistant people, we sometimes have to repeat a gesture or freeze it (hold it in place for a few seconds). As you perform your gesture, be sure to stop and look at the person or group of people whom you are trying to constrain. This will reinforce to them that you mean business.

Table 6.1: Gestures for Reinforcing Framing Statements

Gesture	Effect
Hold out hand in "stop" fashion.	Communicates that you want the person or group to stop talking or to avoid a particular topic
Draw box outline in air with fingers.	Communicates the boundary of the conversation
Hold out hands in front of the body with palms facing inward (in the same manner as some people use to designate length).	Communicates the boundary of the conversation
Hold up fingers to designate "first, second, third," and so on.	Communicates the agenda for the conference or meeting
Move hands in unison to point to one part of the room for 1, another part for 2, another part for 3, and so on.	Communicates the agenda for the conference or meeting

Once you have conveyed the necessary information to the Resident Expert, use the following strategies to ensure that he or she follows your implementation plans:

• Develop written directives and plans.

• Check to make sure the person understands your directions and directives.

- Build in a way to check the person's understanding periodically.
- Set smaller time frames and expectations for plans.
- Use your positional power and authority to elicit compliance.

Figures 6.1 and 6.2 provide some helpful guidelines to follow as you prepare to give directions and to delegate tasks.

The Principal's Role in Creating Resident Experts

Resident Experts can develop their unique skill sets and behaviors all on their own but also may be influenced by some leadership behaviors. In this section, we will examine some ways that administrators can contribute to the development of Resident Experts and will suggest ways to avoid doing so.

- Failing to exhibit strong leadership skills—If a principal is too tentative in explaining an initiative or addressing concerns about it, Resident Experts stand in wait, ready to take up the slack. Be sure that you understand what you are presenting to staff members, and be ready to provide needed clarifications. This will let everyone know that you have done your homework and have enough knowledge to move the initiative forward.

- Giving undo attention to Resident Experts—Sometimes, because Resident Experts sound like they have a good knowledge of a particular area, principals elevate them to leadership positions in the school. Be careful to fully assess staff members' expertise and leadership skills before assigning formal leadership roles on committees and task forces.

- Failing to confront Resident Experts on their ideas—Resident Experts can sound very confident and convincing when they talk, and it can be difficult to ask them for more details or clarification. Appropriately challenge Resident Experts to provide more detail about their claims. This behavior will let them know that you are going to require information to back up what they say.

Working With Staff Members to Deal With Resident Experts

All staff members need to be aware of the issues Resident Experts present when they are not open to direction and learning. Conduct sessions at staff meetings in which you discuss these issues.

Considerations for Giving Directions to Others

It is important to make sure that your directions are clear and easily understood. Keep the following considerations in mind as you prepare to give directions to others:

1. Think through the steps that will be required in order to successfully complete the job or assignment.

2. Arrange the directions in the order that makes the most sense for the successful completion of the job or assignment.

3. Consider the way the person you will be giving the directions to thinks about and processes information. You will want to phrase your directions so that they meet the needs of this person.

4. Before you meet with the other person, put together a preliminary plan—either in your mind or on paper—for how you will deliver the directions.

5. Identify the ways you will ask questions to verify that the person receiving the directions understands what you have asked him or her to do and is ready to move forward on the task.

Figure 6.1: Guidelines for effective directions.

Considerations for Delegating Tasks

In many cases, you will be delegating tasks to others. Delegation can break down because the delegator and the person being given the task may have a different picture of the completed product. Keep the following considerations in mind to ensure that you and the person you are delegating to have the same understanding of the task before it is started.

1. Think about exactly what task you will be delegating to the other person. Make sure you can clearly identify what you want him or her to do.

2. Picture in your mind what you want the completed task to look like when it is finished. Be ready to describe that outcome to the other person.

3. If there are specific steps or stages that need to be followed in a particular order when working on the task, be ready to share them. If not, let the other person know that he or she can determine the steps to complete the task.

4. Identify the strategies or questions you will use to make sure that the person to whom the task is delegated clearly understands what is expected.

5. Identify a date early in the process when you and the other person will meet to talk about short-term progress on the delegated task. This short-term meeting helps both you and the person completing the task ensure that the project is moving in the right direction.

6. Be ready to verify that the person who is working on the delegated task has the necessary resources to complete it.

7. Establish a start and end date for the task.

Figure 6.2: Guidelines for effective delegation.

One of the best ways to help staff members deal with Resident Experts is to hold formal and informal sessions to answer questions about the implementation of the new initiative or strategy. Staff members may generate questions in advance or pose them at the beginning of the meeting. Use any internal expertise that you have on the staff to address the questions that have been raised.

Another helpful strategy is to ask members of the building improvement team to meet with the Resident Experts and connect in a mentoring relationship with them.

"Bridging the Gap" Activity

Resident Experts can undermine the confidence of others on the staff who are working together to implement new ideas and strategies. They do so by pointing out what they perceive to be gaps or problems in an implementation. If the rest of your staff starts to think that you have not considered all aspects of your initiative or project, the Resident Experts' influence grows, and their behavior is reinforced. An activity called "Bridging the Gap" can counter the Resident Experts' influence by highlighting the connections between your old and new ways of doing business, thus ensuring a smooth transition.

In this activity, staff members identify the attributes of the new program or initiative and consider the similarities to other, more familiar experiences. Going through this process helps staff members begin to develop a pathway between the old ways and the new change or initiative.

Here is how the activity works:

1   The meeting leader talks to the staff as a whole about the importance of bridging the gap between existing practices, or the old way of doing things, and the new change or initiative.

2   The large group is divided into smaller subgroups and given the worksheet shown in figure 6.3. Visit **go.solution-tree.com/leadership** to download this worksheet.

3   The small groups are asked to generate a list of five to six attributes or requirements of the new program or initiative. They write these points down in column 1 on the worksheet. For example, if the new initiative is response to intervention (RTI), an attribute or a requirement might be "Gathering informal assessment data to help make decisions about a student's progress toward the learning objectives." For differentiated instruction, an attribute or a requirement might be "Diagnosing each student's preferred learning styles or strategies."

4 Once these ideas have been compiled, the groups engage in conversations to identify elements of past initiatives that are similar to or the same as elements of the new program or initiative. They then list the similarities or commonalities in column 2 on the worksheet.

5 Finally, the small groups engage in conversations about how they will use the similarities or commonalities in column 2 to help them implement the requirements of the new program or initiative. They record these strategies in column 3.

6 The large group reconvenes. Each of the small groups presents its chart and ideas to the large group. The large group discusses what has been learned as a result of this activity and how it will help the staff bridge the gap between the old or existing processes and the new programs or initiatives.

Bridging the Gap

Use this worksheet to generate strategies and ideas to help you make a successful transition from an old or existing practice to a new idea or practice.

1. Name the new practice, program, or initiative.

2. Discuss the topics presented in the table, and list your ideas about them in the appropriate columns.

Attributes or requirements of the new initiative	Similarities or commonalities between the new requirements and elements of other familiar programs	Strategies for using the similarities or commonalities identified in column 2 to assist in the implementation of the new program or initiative

3. What have we learned as a result of this activity?

4. How will this learning help us be successful as we move forward with the new program or initiative?

Figure 6.3: Worksheet for "Bridging the Gap" activity.

Without effectively managing transitions, you may unknowingly be developing a new group of difficult or resistant people. As you work with Resident Experts, understanding how they have traveled through past transitions in the workplace may give you some insights into why they are so negative. Armed with this information, you'll be better able to help them develop and implement a plan to change their behaviors.

Summary

Resident Experts may seem innocent enough in terms of their impact on your school climate and culture, but because of their lack of interest in listening and learning, they can be dangerous. If you allow their behavior to continue unchecked, others on your staff may begin to think that they, too, can get away with not complying with your directives regarding new initiatives. This could create an unhealthy atmosphere in which everyone is doing his or her own thing rather than working together as a united team to improve the school and student achievement. If you end up with a bunch of independent contractors, you will experience trouble moving forward on any initiative.

Another danger of failing to rein in Resident Experts is that others on the staff will eventually figure out that these people don't know what they are talking about. Their professional credibility will suffer, and they will not be able to collaborate properly with other staff members. This situation further erodes your efforts to have the staff function as a team. It is clear that letting Resident Experts go on with their behaviors without redirection will cause you trouble and make your school more difficult to lead.

Questions for Reflection

What are the characteristics and behaviors of Resident Experts?

Who are the Resident Experts on your staff? What behaviors do they exhibit that inform you that they are Resident Experts?

How do Resident Experts negatively affect the rest of your staff? How do they diminish the climate and culture of your school?

What are some techniques and strategies that you can use to change the behaviors of Resident Experts?

How can you as the principal personally confront Resident Experts and hold them accountable for their assertions?

chapter 7

The Unelected Representatives

Some staff members take it upon themselves to speak for others on your staff. You may see these "Unelected Representatives" appear in a variety of situations. If left unchecked, they can move from being unofficial spokespersons to becoming official spokespersons. Their influence can be powerful and destructive. You need to attack their behaviors immediately.

As you read this chapter, you will learn the following:

- Typical behaviors of Unelected Representatives

- Strategies for handling Unelected Representatives

- The principal's role in creating Unelected Representatives

- Ways to help develop the skills of other staff members to effectively deal with Unelected Representatives and minimize their impact

Behaviors of Unelected Representatives

When Unelected Representatives speak for others, they begin to gain power and influence and can actually have the effect of silencing others. Here are some of the specific behaviors we have seen Unelected Representatives engage in:

- Working to stir up negative sentiment against the change or new initiative

- Maintaining that they are trying to ensure that things are fair and equitable for other staff members; insisting that if they don't speak for these staff members, nobody else will

- Expressing anti-administration views

- Being in everyone's business all the time

Let's look at a situation in which a principal finds that she is dealing with an Unelected Representative.

Scenario: The Staff Author

When she assumes the principalship at Adams Elementary School, Annette is excited to get started. As she looks through her mail, she sees a letter from one of her teachers, Bernie. In the letter, Bernie tells her how dissatisfied he is with her appointment and says that the other staff members agree with him. This obviously troubles her, and as she begins to assess the situation, she decides she needs to gather some data informally. She starts to observe Bernie's interactions with and influence over his colleagues. She notices that when Bernie makes comments, few staff members challenge him, even though she knows his comments do not match what her teachers are telling her privately. She decides that she needs to address the situation.

Annette arranges to meet with Bernie to discuss his letter. As she talks with him, she asks him to give her examples of his specific concerns, but he is unwilling to do so. She puts him on notice that if he has a concern in the future, he will need to meet with her personally rather than write a letter or try to get others on the faculty involved in his issues.

Annette also spends individual time with other selected faculty members to help them learn how to share their own concerns. She couches this training in terms of strategies for dealing with disagreeable parents. She begins to notice that some key members of her staff are gaining confidence and are starting to be able to stand up for their own views rather than just blindly following along.

This process comes together for the first time at a faculty meeting, right after Annette introduces a new idea. In the middle of the discussion, Bernie says, "I don't agree with this idea. I know there are many others on the staff who share my feelings."

Annette is ready for this situation and replies, "This has not been my experience in my interactions with other staff members." She has planned an activity that will give everyone an opportunity to express his or her true feelings. "I want you to talk in pairs about your positive and negative perceptions of the idea that I shared in today's meeting and write your thoughts on a piece of paper." The groups talk for about five minutes and then present their perceptions of the idea. They mention both the positive aspects of the idea and their concerns about it. Annette writes down all of their points and tells the group that she will consider them and give her responses at the next staff meeting.

Lessons From This Scenario

Unelected Representatives work hard to speak for others and to undermine your confidence. It's important for you to recognize that they *don't* speak for the people they say they do. Becoming aware of their manipulative efforts is one of the first steps you can take to defeat those efforts.

What would you do if you received an email or a letter like the one Annette got from Bernie? Here are some suggested actions, many of which we saw Annette performing:

- After reading the message, take a few minutes to think about the fact you are being manipulated.

- Look for vague and nonspecific information in the message that is designed to make you feel that everyone on the staff is against you. Ask yourself about the feasibility of these comments. If you come across statements like the following, be careful in your interpretation:
    - "Many on our staff feel this way but have asked me to address the situation."
    - "Others have been talking but were afraid to come forward. I am speaking for them."
    - "We all feel that . . ."

- Rather than try to rationalize the message, set up a meeting with the person who wrote it to talk through the issues. He or she may be counting on the fact that few people actually confront acts like this. In most cases, leaders just file the information away and never actually check on the accuracy of the message.

- Informally check with other staff members to find out their feelings and perceptions about the general themes addressed in the message. You may find some truth to the writer's claims, but usually most staff members don't agree with the thoughts in such a message.

Further Strategies for Handling Unelected Representatives

As we have mentioned, the Unelected Representative can become a destructive force who works to undermine your leadership and your efforts to improve the school climate and culture. If left unchecked, this person can begin to make others on the staff come around to his or her way of thinking.

Here are some ideas to address the behaviors and attitudes of Unelected Representatives:

- Carefully watch the behaviors of your staff members so that you can identify potential Unelected Representatives. If you notice that someone has the potential to become an Unelected Representative, stay close to this person so you can observe how he or she goes about developing relationships with other staff members.

- Make sure you are providing accurate and timely information to *everyone* on your staff to minimize the anxiety level of your staff members. This will keep them from confiding in Unelected Representatives.

- Develop and implement a proactive method for staff members to share concerns with you and get their concerns resolved. This will prevent the Unelected Representatives from gaining a hold on your staff.

- When you receive information from an Unelected Representative, listen carefully to see if you can pick up patterns in the message. Look for vague or unsubstantiated information designed to make you draw conclusions or become nervous or paranoid.

- Ask Unelected Representatives to share the specifics of their vague or general message. Driving them to specificity normally takes the wind out of their sails and diminishes their manipulative message.

- Talk to other staff members whom the person contends he or she represents. Ask them if they truly feel that the Unelected Representative speaks for them.

- Make it a regular practice to meet with staff members individually so that they can give you their feedback or share any concerns they have. Be open to their concerns, and don't react negatively when they share their thoughts.

- Inform the Unelected Representatives that they cannot speak for others on the staff. Tell them you are interested only in hearing from each staff member directly about any concerns related to the new initiative.

- Post a concerns chart in the faculty lounge, in the room for staff meetings, or in other professional development facilities as a place for staff members to record their concerns.

- Install a suggestion box that staff members can use to share their concerns.

- Be on the lookout for implementation blocking (see the following discussion).

Implementation Blocking

Unelected Representatives are frequently engaging in what is known as "implementation blocking." Here is a brief definition: *Implementation blocking is a process whereby an individual or a group tries to slow or block a change through the use of comments that undermine the confidence of the leader.* For example, an Unelected Representative might tell you that he or she knows that many people have concerns about your leadership or initiative. The intent is to make you uncomfortable or even to get you to back down on your initiative.

You can take several steps to deal with implementation blocking:

- Recognize that implementation blocking is happening.

- Listen to the message, ask clarification questions, and seek to understand the nature and origin of the concern.

- Listen for the core of the concern.

- Listen for specific language; be careful about vague or general statements.

Table 7.1 gives examples of statements that signal implementation blocking, explains what the speaker hopes to accomplish with the statements, and offers ways for leaders to respond to the statements.

Table 7.1: Implementation Blocking Statements

Statement	Manipulation	Response
"Many of us on the staff are wondering why this initiative went forward without more discussion."	The speaker is trying to make the leader question the involvement process he or she used for the decision.	Ask the speaker to specifically identify who the people are and what they are concerned about.
"I've been talking to other staff and parents who share my concerns . . ."	The speaker is trying to make the leader think that a lot of people are upset and are on the side of the speaker.	Ask the speaker to share who the staff members and parents are and what concerns they have. Possibly follow up with these people to gain their perspective.
"The informal leaders of the building met and have talked about what is wrong with this project."	The speaker is trying to make the leader think that there is a group that is meeting behind his or her back about the issue. This can make the leader paranoid and nervous.	Ask the speaker for more specifics; let everyone know you will set up a meeting with the informal leaders to hear their concerns.

Source: Adapted from Eller (2004).

The Principal's Role in Creating Unelected Representatives

Principals can inadvertently reinforce or even increase the behaviors of Unelected Representatives. In this section, we will look at some of the common ways this happens and suggest appropriate counterstrategies.

- Listening to and acting on the assertions of Unelected Representatives without checking their validity or accuracy—If an Unelected Representative tells you that others feel a certain way about something, make this person tell you specifically what people are saying and who is actually saying it. Then follow through on the assertions in a positive but prompt manner. Until other staff members tell you something directly, consider the Unelected Representative's statements to be hearsay.

- Failing to allow discussions of all sides of the issues before implementation—Hold open forums in which staff members are allowed to share both the positive and negative aspects of issues under consideration. Help the staff develop strategies and ideas for addressing their areas of concern, or pull back on the new initiative until the concerns can be addressed.

- Being an autocratic leader and squelching conversation—Provide different vehicles for staff members to use in airing their ideas and concerns, such as confidential surveys, a school suggestion box, or focus groups and interviews conducted by outside facilitators. When they are free to express their own views, staff members don't have to rely on Unelected Representatives to carry their concerns forward.

Working With Staff Members to Deal With Unelected Representatives

One of the best ways to keep Unelected Representatives at bay is to develop a set of working norms with your staff. Working norms often focus on communication and interaction. They make explicit the conditions that staff members need for a positive working environment. The "What Do We Expect?" activity can help start the process of developing norms.

"What Do We Expect?" Activity

This activity (Eller & Eller, 2009) can be used when a new principal arrives, when a new initiative is brought forward, or whenever expectations need to be clarified. Here is how it works:

1 The principal gathers all staff members together to talk about the importance of clear expectations.

2 The staff members are subdivided into smaller groups of five to six people.

3 Each of the groups is asked to respond to the following questions and record its answers on chart paper:

- What do we expect from our leader? (Possible answers might be "To be open and honest with us . . . to work with us to build a great team . . . to use her knowledge of teaching and learning to help us grow as professionals.")

- What do we expect from our faculty members and team members? (Possible answers might be "To pitch in and support each other as a team . . . to listen to each other's ideas before disagreeing or making a decision . . . to respect each other as professionals.")

- What do we expect from ourselves as individuals? (Possible answers might be "To come to work each day prepared and ready to teach . . . to accept others and their ideas . . . to listen to get to know others . . . to be aware of the impact my comments and actions have on other team members.")

4 Once all the groups have completed their lists, they are asked to report out their work.

5 After each group reports out its list, the principal asks the large group to summarize what was said and to start keeping track of what the lists have in common.

6 Once all of the groups have reported out their lists, the principal shares his or her expectations of the staff. The principal asks the small teams to meet again and talk about the expectations. Each team is asked to talk about expectations that its members cannot live with if they are enacted at the school.

7   Once each team reports out on its latest discussion, a list that reflects the combined expectations is created, printed out, and distributed at a future faculty meeting for comments and final adoption.

Faculty Advisory Council

Another strategy that is effective in keeping staff members from relying on Unelected Representatives is to establish a faculty advisory council. The council can work like this:

- Faculty members select a group of their colleagues to serve on the faculty advisory council.

- The council should include membership from the major groups or divisions of the school.

- Positions on the council should include the chair, a secretary or note taker, a facilitator, and any other roles that the group feels would help it be more effective in its operation.

- Any staff member who has a concern is asked to submit it in writing to the chair of the council.

- The chair of the council meets with the principal to discuss the concern and to allow the principal time to reflect on it before it is submitted to the council as a whole.

- The entire faculty advisory council meets once a month to discuss the concerns and to help resolve them positively for the faculty member who submitted them and for any others who are affected by them.

Professional Development and Support

While the faculty advisory council should minimize the influence of Unelected Representatives, you should nonetheless spend time with your staff members teaching them to stand up for themselves if they are ever pressured by such people. You can frame this professional development in the more general context of learning skills to become more assertive and confident in communications with others.

Finally, you can meet privately with and offer support to those staff members who wish to confront the Unelected Representatives on the staff.

Summary

Like other difficult and resistant staff members, Unelected Representatives can have a negative impact on you as the leader and on your school improvement initiatives. These people and their behaviors can develop as a result of many factors but are reinforced by faculty members who don't have the ability to state their own opinions or are afraid to do so. Understanding how Unelected Representatives succeed in spreading their influence can keep you from being caught off guard.

When you discover someone who is inclined to take on this role within your staff, you need to move quickly both to strengthen the rest of the staff and to destabilize the Unelected Representative. In this chapter, you have learned strategies and ideas that can help you accomplish both tasks. Remember that the longer you allow Unelected Representatives to continue their behavior, the harder it will be for you to counter their influence over your staff. The sooner you intervene, the better chance you have of neutralizing their impact and developing a healthy school climate and culture.

Questions for Reflection

What staff members at your school are possibly Unelected Representatives? Who might be predisposed to become an Unelected Representative if the conditions were right? How might you be able to head off this development and build the skills of the rest of the staff members so they don't need to rely on Unelected Representatives?

How do Unelected Representatives gain their power and respect? What may be happening on your staff that is contributing to their success?

What ideas and strategies can you employ to begin to break down Unelected Representatives' hold on the staff? How can you use the information they provide to gain more clarity and specificity related to the concerns and the staff members they profess to represent?

chapter 8

The Whiners and Complainers

We know this type of difficult school employee well. We hear from the Whiners and Complainers on a regular basis, especially when things don't work well for them. For some Whiners and Complainers, this means that we hear from them all the time. They are so relentless in their feedback about what is not going well for them that we tend to discount what they are saying.

As you read this chapter, you will learn the following:

- The typical behaviors of Whiners and Complainers
- Strategies for handling Whiners and Complainers
- The principal's role in creating Whiners and Complainers
- Ways to help develop the skills of other staff members to effectively deal with Whiners and Complainers in their midst

Behaviors of Whiners and Complainers

Here are some behaviors that are typical of Whiners and Complainers:

- These people find fault with everything. Somehow, no matter how much you do for them, they always need more.
- If there is an issue or a problem in their classroom, they pass it off as someone else's fault. They blame their issues on other staff members, parents, and students.
- Whiners and Complainers have difficulty in seeing their part or role in making a situation successful.
- When presented with an idea or a strategy, Whiners and Complainers will naturally focus on why it won't work, the obstacles that could get in its way, and what they don't have that they need to be successful.

- Whiners and Complainers will immediately find fault in you and your leadership.

- Whiners and Complainers may bring up multiple issues at one time, issues from the past, or issues outside of their or your ability to control. This behavior tends to keep the situation destabilized and in play. If you are able to solve an issue, they lose their ability to complain.

Because they are always negative and pessimistic, Whiners and Complainers have a way of alienating other staff members and you as their leader. Their attitude can rub off on others, causing them to become negative and pessimistic. When they have affected a critical mass of the staff, the climate and culture of the school can become negative and pessimistic.

Let's see how one principal deals with an incident in which Whiners and Complainers threaten to derail a staff meeting.

Scenario: That Won't Work

Karen, a high school principal, is meeting with her staff to talk about a new advisee program. In the middle of her description of the program, a small group of three people speaks up, pointing out the flaws of the new plan and listing the resources they are missing that will keep them from being successful. As they continue to criticize the program, others on the staff start to join in on the complaint session. If the complaining continues, the entire meeting could get out of control.

Karen stops the meeting and says to the group, "Obviously, some of you have issues with the new program. I want you to get into groups and talk about the advisee program." Karen has the teachers number off, and then she puts them into random groups. She asks each group to generate lists in response to the following questions:

- What seems to be working well in relation to the advisee program?

- What is not working well in relation to the advisee program?

- How do we want to work together to overcome those things that are not working well with the program?

After the groups generate their initial lists, she has them report out their information. Some of the groups return to the same challenges the Whiners and Complainers brought up earlier in the meeting, but they also offer lists of strategies they could use to overcome those challenges. Instead of being consumed by the challenges, the groups are able to figure out their own strategies to be successful.

Lessons From This Scenario

Karen decided she needed to put a stop to the negative energy that was beginning to develop as a result of the Whiners and Complainers at her meeting. She knew that her staff members had the capacity to solve their own issues, so she came up with a way to steer them in that direction. Karen's solution fit the group's strengths and the building culture.

Here are additional ideas for dealing with a scenario like this one:

- Connect with the Whiners and Complainers to assess their issues and complaints. Listen and try to get them to be more specific about their thoughts and concerns.

- Check the accuracy of complaints with other staff members. Karen asked for her staff members' perceptions immediately because she had already informally checked with some of them before the meeting about potential issues. She was relatively sure that she knew the major issues and could guide the staff beyond them.

- Help the staff members develop a proactive response to the major issues rather than let the Whiners and Complainers influence them into thinking the sky is falling.

Further Strategies for Handling Whiners and Complainers

The best strategies to use with Whiners and Complainers are those that help them see things from another perspective or look at them in a different manner. There are several ways to redirect their thinking.

Seeing the Big Picture

Work with Whiners and Complainers to help them broaden their focus. You might ask a probing question that will lead them to think about what will happen over the longer term ("How do you see your issue impacting the school five years from now?") or help them see the larger context of the situation ("At this point you've identified an issue that applies to this graduating class. How do you see it impacting the rest of the school?"). Reflecting or paraphrasing is a good way to help Whiners and Complainers look at an issue from a different processing level than the one they are now stuck in. For example, you might observe, "You're stuck in the mud on this issue" (reflecting the person's emotional state) or "You see this at the micro level right now. It may look different from ten thousand feet up" (setting a broader context).

Framing

Earlier in this book, we introduced the skill of framing. In framing, you set the parameters that you will accept for the conversation. These kinds of statements work very well with Whiners and Complainers and help to constrict their conversations. Here are some examples:

- "I know that in previous conversations, you wanted to spend time talking about how you were treated unfairly in the past, but in this conversation today, we will concentrate only on what we will do in the future."

- "As we work together in generating ideas to address your concerns, we need to stay away from things we cannot control, like the backgrounds of your students."

- "I'll listen to what you think is wrong, but I won't listen to any negative comments about your colleagues."

If you frame conversations, it helps to keep Whiners and Complainers focused on tangible issues that hold the potential to be resolved.

Reframing

Reframing is another effective technique for changing the Whiners' and Complainers' focus. Reframing sounds like this:

- "You've mentioned the weaknesses of the program. What strengths do you see in the program that can help us as a school?"

- "If you were to look at this from the perspective of a parent, what differences would you see?"

- "If we were able to eliminate your concerns, how do you see the program moving forward?"

An exercise called "Reframing Your View" (fig. 8.1) takes Whiners and Complainers through a process that helps them look at things differently. Visit **go.solution-tree.com/leadership** to download this exercise.

Integration Reflecting

In many cases, Whiners and Complainers have trouble focusing on exactly what is bothering them because they have so many unresolved issues. Not only are they upset about the new idea, they are upset about the fact that the old strategy they liked will soon be gone. They might be having a hard time accepting the imminent retirement of a colleague, they could be lamenting

Reframing Your View

1. Reflect on a problem that may be facing you; clarify the details of the problem.

2. Define the potential impact of the problem.

3. Define how you might possibly cause, influence, or perpetuate the problem.

4. Lay out the worst-case scenario if the problem comes to pass. Decide if you can survive the worst-case scenario.

5. Design a plan to address the worst-case scenario if the problem comes to pass. This plan should also help you as you work proactively to prevent the problem.

Figure 8.1: Exercise to help staff members reframe a problem.

the fact that they are getting older, and so on. You can help Whiners and Complainers address their issues and move forward by using a technique called "integration reflecting." This technique allows you to put their concerns into a nice, neat package so they are able to see them and address them. Here is how it works:

1   Engage in a private conversation with the Whiner or Complainer. Ask this person to tell you exactly what is bothering him or her. Be sure to let the person know this is a confidential, no-penalty conversation.

2   Tell the Whiner or Complainer to share *all* of his or her concerns with you. Ask the person to go back and replay the concerns from the beginning.

3   Listen carefully as the person describes his or her concerns. Listen for multiple complaints or issues of concern. In your mind, track those concerns, and look for patterns or connections between them.

4   When the concerns are all out on the table, use a reflecting statement to sum up what you heard. When delivering reflecting statements, you give a clear and direct summary without adding in your interpretation or judgment. Here are some examples of possible integration reflecting statements:

   - "Over the years, you have experienced a lack of organization when new initiatives have been started."

   - "You expressed many things that are bothering you. They all revolve around your feeling that your ideas aren't respected by the rest of the faculty."

   - "Your concerns seem to fit into three general themes. First, the idea we are working on has not been field-tested. Second, there seems to be a lack of respect for what has been done here in the past. Third, this idea does not take into account the needs of the teachers."

   - "In general, your major thoughts all revolve around the idea that we need to slow down in our implementation of the new program."

5   Once you make the integration reflecting statement, you will see if you have sufficiently identified and addressed the staff member's concerns. If you have, you will see a relaxed look come over his or her face, and the person may even reply with a comment like "Yes, that's it exactly!" or "You hit the nail on the head." Once you have addressed the person's major concern, you can now work with him or her through further conversation, questioning, or planning.

The Principal's Role in Creating Whiners and Complainers

Principals may inadvertently or unknowingly create or reinforce Whiners and Complainers in their school. In this section, we will look at some of the common ways they do so and suggest the appropriate counterstrategies.

   - Providing attention that meets the needs of Whiners and Complainers—Principals who respond immediately to Whiners and

Complainers give them the reinforcement they need to continue their behavior. Try to resist the impulse to quickly satisfy these staff members' needs. Direct them back to the source of their complaint, or ask them to research its background before you will engage with them. This strategy makes them think through things before just venting to you.

- Allowing Whiners and Complainers to monopolize staff meeting time—Whiners and Complainers can be notorious for holding up meetings in order to get their point across. Limit the amount of time that Whiners and Complainers are allowed to have the floor during staff meetings. When they have reached their time limit, politely redirect the group back to the agenda. If this strategy doesn't work, consider more direct or forceful approaches.

- Allowing Whiners and Complainers to present unsubstantiated information—At times, Whiners and Complainers go on about things that simply are not true. Before you allow them to carry on, ask these difficult staff members to substantiate their complaints. This strategy will reduce their impulse to complain, as well as reveal the source of their information. If the information they are upset about is true, it may be worth a group conversation.

- Dismissing or ignoring the comments of Whiners and Complainers—We have found that some Whiners and Complainers go on and on because they believe that they have to engage in this behavior in order to be heard by others. Over the years, people have just dismissed their thoughts and ideas. If you reflect or paraphrase the content or emotions of their whining and complaining, it lets them feel heard and may diminish their negative behavior.

- Not providing feedback to Whiners and Complainers—Not many staff members are excited about taking on the Whiners and Complainers or providing feedback to them about the negative impact they have on the staff. You may need to sit down with the Whiners and Complainers and have a frank and open conversation with them about your perceptions of their behavior. As a part of this conversation, you may want to talk with them about strategies they can use to get their point across without being perceived as a Whiner and Complainer.

Working With Staff Members to Handle Whiners and Complainers

All staff members need to be able to recognize the behaviors of Whiners and Complainers. Hold a conversation at a staff meeting in which you talk through these behaviors and stress their negative impact on others in the organization. Point out the ineffectiveness of whining and complaining in getting things accomplished. Ask staff members to help one another in providing feedback and redirection when they see a colleague whining and complaining.

Group Norms

If you feel the staff has the strength and capacity to set group norms, use an all-staff meeting to develop a group norm against whining and complaining. Such a norm might be worded as follows:

> As a staff we will focus on dealing productively with our problems rather than whining or complaining about them.

If you think the staff is not ready for this step, set up a ground rule (a directive that you establish without the participation of the staff) that prohibits whining and complaining. For example:

> There will be no whining or complaining tolerated here.

Learning to Talk With Whiners and Complainers

One of the things Whiners and Complainers count on is that they will not be asked or confronted about the details of their complaints. Most other people on the staff have learned to just ignore them and to try to get away without further discussion. But this strategy only reinforces their continued whining and complaining. It's a good idea to actually teach staff members how to talk with Whiners and Complainers to find out exactly what is bothering them and to offer their opinions if they are comfortable doing so. We have developed guidelines that staff members can use for these conversations:

- When the Whiners and Complainers start to talk, temporarily suspend your opinion, and try to truly listen to what they are saying. As you are listening, formulate questions you may want to ask them to get more specifics about their issues.

- After they have shared their concerns, respond by asking a clarifying question that drives the Whiners and Complainers to specificity. Here are some sample questions:

- "What specific evidence have you seen that helped you determine that this was true?"

- "What examples can you share that back up your assertions?"

- "How did you determine that this was happening?"

- When the Whiners and Complainers respond, listen to what they say to see if they address the question you asked. If they do, determine if the information they provide is valid or is still vague or general. If necessary, ask another focusing question.

- If you determine that their complaint is unfounded or based on incomplete evidence, ask for more clarity, let them know you disagree with their conceptualization of the idea, or direct them to the party who will help them get their issues resolved.

It is also helpful to teach staff members the techniques we recommended earlier for redirecting the thinking of Whiners and Complainers: reframing and reflecting their issues.

"Sweet and Sour Memories" Activity

At times, Whiners and Complainers have gotten that way because they feel that they are being asked to move forward with a new idea before they are able to let go of an old behavior or practice. They can also long for the "good old days" because they fear setting out into unknown territory. We have found that a good way to help people let go of their attachment to the past and begin to move forward in accepting a new idea or initiative is to allow them to see that the old way of doing things wasn't as good as they think.

An activity called "Sweet and Sour Memories" gives staff members an opportunity to talk about the good things and the not-so-good things about the practice that is being phased out. This allows an important mental process to occur—it is the beginning of transitioning out of the old and preparing for the new—and helps keep people from becoming negative and difficult. It also gives you insight into the emotions behind resistance to new ideas or strategies.

Here are the steps for implementing this activity:

1 Hand out the worksheet for the activity "Sweet and Sour Memories" (fig. 8.2, page 92).

2 Have staff members spend five to ten minutes reflecting on and recording their memories of the practice or program that is being phased out.

Sweet and Sour Memories

An important part of the change process is honoring the past. Please take a few minutes to write down your thoughts regarding the terminating program or process at our school. After you complete your thoughts, you will be sharing your memories in a small group.

1. Name the project, program, or practice that is no longer going to be used.

2. List your memories of the program or practice in columns 1 and 2. Do not complete column 3 until after our large-group conversation.

"Sweet" memories or positive aspects of this program or practice	"Sour" memories or irritating or somewhat negative aspects of this program or practice	Ideas or strategies to replace the sweet memories or positive aspects once this program or practice is gone

Figure 8.2: Worksheet for "Sweet and Sour Memories" activity.

3   Once most people have completed the first two columns of the worksheet, have everyone meet in groups of three to four to talk about their positive and not-so-positive memories. Allow people to choose which memories to share with others in the group.

4   At the end of the sharing session, ask each group to complete a tally listing the positive and negative emotions that its members identified. Also, ask the groups to be ready to share their discussions of highlights of, generalizations about, or impressions of the activity or practice that is being phased out.

5   Reconvene the large group, and let each group share its tallies and impressions. Conduct a large-group conversation about the activity and the impressions of the old practice or program. As the facilitator of this activity, you should try to keep the discussion from crossing the line between reminiscing about the terminating practice or program and "whining" about it.

6 As a closure activity, ask the small groups to meet again to talk about what they or the school can do to replace the good attributes of the terminating process or program.

When we have conducted this activity, we have seen a variety of responses during the large-group processing. Figure 8.3 (page 94) is a sample completed worksheet, which shows some of the memories people can come up with.

"Letting Go" Activity

We have seen that Whiners and Complainers can sometimes have great difficulty letting go of the past. They will cling not only to programs that are ending but also to comments that have been made to them. We have encountered Whiners and Complainers who have hung on to negative comments from others for years.

The "Letting Go" activity is somewhat related to the previous activity and is used primarily to provide a strong emotional break with the terminating program or practice. We have also used it when people were having trouble letting go of negative comments or difficult situations with their colleagues. It works wonders in helping individuals and groups release negative emotions and move forward in a more positive manner. It is ceremonial in nature and can elicit strong feelings. Here is how to conduct this activity:

1 At a meeting, have staff members gather to talk about the strengths and weaknesses of the terminating program or practice.

2 Ask the staff members to write down their perceptions of the positives and negatives on small slips of paper.

3 Gather up the slips of paper that contain negatives.

4 Place the negative slips of paper in a fireproof container. Then burn them. (Be careful when burning the slips; you may want to do it outside.)

5 Once the slips are burned, have the rest of the faculty accompany you outside to bury the ashes.

Because the slips are burned and the ashes buried, it can become harder for staff members to figuratively hold on to the old behaviors and practices. We have conducted ceremonies like this with great success. The activity is included here because it can be implemented with an entire staff or a small group and may help everyone to deal with the issues that Whiners and Complainers bring to the whole staff.

Sweet and Sour Memories

An important part of the change process is honoring the past. Please take a few minutes to write down your thoughts regarding the terminating program or process at our school. After you complete your thoughts, you will be sharing your memories in a small group.

1. Name the project, program, or practice that is no longer going to be used.

Students being required to qualify in order to take Advanced Placement courses here at the high school. In the past, students were required to get teacher recommendations, develop a position paper, and have As in other courses before being allowed to sign up for AP courses.

2. List your memories of the program or practice in columns 1 and 2. Do not complete column 3 until after our large-group conversation.

"Sweet" memories or positive aspects of this program or practice	"Sour" memories or irritating or somewhat negative aspects of this program or practice	Ideas or strategies to replace the sweet memories or positive aspects once this program or practice is gone
This seemed to help us get students who were more committed to working hard in AP courses.	*Someone had to read all of the papers that students submitted when they applied for program entry.*	*Staff members can still advise and work with students who are considering AP placement.*
Teachers had some control over who could take AP courses.	*We had to deal with the parents of those students who didn't get a chance to try to get into these courses.*	*AP teachers can meet with all of the students and parents of students who are interested in their program to talk about the rigors of the courses and get a commitment that the students understand the difficulties and are willing to do the extra work it may take in order to be successful in the program.*
The numbers in our courses were manageable.	*We always thought that some students with good potential were overlooked because they had a few lower grades in other courses.*	*Students who might not have been obvious candidates can be given a chance to take advantage of new learning opportunities.*

Figure 8.3: Sample completed worksheet.

Summary

Whiners and Complainers can cause serious trouble at your school. It's important that you quickly respond to their issues and help the rest of the staff members see that some of their issues are not as serious as they portray in their spirited complaints. In this chapter, we have provided you with techniques and strategies to meet these difficult people at their level and begin to address some of their whining and complaining behavior. These ideas and strategies have been time-tested and will work to stop the spread of pessimism and negativity.

Questions for Reflection

What are the typical behaviors of Whiners and Complainers? How do they try to get your and other staff members' attention by using these behaviors?

How do the strategies of reframing and reflecting help Whiners and Complainers see their issues from other angles?

What have you learned in this chapter that you can put into immediate use in working with the Whiners and Complainers in your organization?

chapter 9

Defending Yourself and Next Steps

De
Ne

So far in this book, we have presented strategies to address specific types of difficult and resistant people you may encounter on your staff. In this chapter, we will look at two practices that are crucial for your success in dealing with anyone who is working to block or hold up your change efforts: self-protection and follow-up. You will learn:

- Self-protection strategies to keep you from absorbing the negative energy of difficult and resistant staff members and retreating from your efforts to confront them

- Strategies to plan and perform follow-up to ensure that the difficult and resistant behaviors you have worked hard to address stay addressed

- Steps to take to keep your project or initiative positive and on track after it is launched

Self-Protection

When you are in confrontational situations, you are open to attack. You can choose from a variety of techniques and strategies to divert or block the negative energy emitted during confrontations and protect yourself psychologically. Diversion or self-protection strategies are highly personal in nature. Some will work for you, while others will make you uncomfortable. It is crucial for you to think through and assess your skills and needs before you decide to take on the difficult or resistant people in your school. If you go into the task without adequate preparation and planning, you could get overwhelmed and in trouble quickly. Knowing your skills and comfort level in confronting difficult or resistant people can help you gain confidence and the resolve not to take any negative feedback they provide. We recommend conducting the self-assessment offered in table 9.1. Visit **go.solution-tree .com/leadership** to download this tool.

Table 9.1: Confrontation Skills Self-Assessment

Skill	Your Level of Skill (E = Emerging, C = Competent, P = Proficient)	Evidence for Rating	Strategy or Resource Needed to Improve Skill or Confidence
Accuracy in describing difficult or resistant behavior of staff member			
Precision in planning a confrontational conference			
Confidence in telling employee the issue at hand			
Ability to keep conversation focused on the issue when the staff member tries to sidetrack the conversation			
Ability to deliver directives to stop negative behaviors			
Knowledge of the possible consequences available to you for the difficult employee			
Ability to handle the pressures from other faculty members if the difficult or resistant staff member enlists their help or assistance			

Let's see how one well-prepared principal approaches a confrontational meeting with a difficult staff member.

Scenario: The Overpowering Staff Member

As she prepares to confront David, a difficult and negative staff member at her middle school, Jan, the principal, is understandably nervous. She has seen David in confrontations with other staff members and even parents. David has a take-no-prisoners approach in his dealings with others. His goal in confrontations is to try to overpower the other party so he can win. He normally accomplishes this through techniques such as "getting in people's faces" and raising his voice to intimidate them. Jan has seen David use this behavior repeatedly in the past and is ready for him when their conference begins.

She has decided to meet with David in her office, since it is her turf. She has raised her chair several inches so that she will be sitting eye to eye with David. She has also written her concerns on a sheet of paper so that she can share them with him during the conference.

After a brief opening, Jan presents her concerns about David's negativity. She uses the piece of paper with the list of concerns as a visual aid for the conference. She holds it out in front of both herself and David so that the focus will be on the paper (and her concerns) rather than on her personally. This technique seems to help David stay calm and listen to Jan's ideas. At one point in the conference, however, David starts to get agitated. Jan makes a "stop" gesture (hand held out with palm facing David) and tells him to stop. He immediately begins to get calm again. As Jan delivers the rest of her comments, she keeps her words simple and direct. She refers to her position as David's supervisor when she presents her directives for him to change his behavior. Finally, Jan shares her plan to follow up and ensure that David gets assistance with his growth task. Having communicated her concerns and expectations, Jan adjourns the conference.

As she reflects back on the experience, Jan is pleasantly surprised that she was able to implement techniques that calmed the situation and helped to protect her emotionally from David's attacks.

Techniques to Divert Negative Energy

It may seem like Jan's ability to control David's emotions and protect herself during the conference in the scenario just described was magical and something that would be difficult to do. In reality, self-protection skills are basic and somewhat intuitive in nature. Most people can learn them and effectively apply them in potentially negative or confrontational situations.

In our scenario, we saw that Jan put in place several techniques to help her survive and thrive. When she made her chair taller, she was evening the playing field in terms of physical size. By writing her concerns on paper and then using that paper as a visual aid, Jan changed the focus from herself to the concerns. Finally, when David's emotions appeared to be escalating, Jan used a gesture to reestablish control.

Here are some other strategies we have used ourselves and taught others to use when they are charged with confronting difficult or resistant people:

- Positive self-talk for internal emotional control—When you confront difficult or resistant staff members, controlling your emotional state is very important for your success. Practice positive self-talk (self-encouragement) as a way to help you stay calm, assertive, on track, focused, and less susceptible to attack.

- Knowing where your project or initiative is going—Thinking through your project or initiative and trying to identify potential pitfalls or bumps in the road can help you answer questions and address concerns more quickly and confidently.

- Framing conversations—Using the framing strategies that we presented earlier in this book (see pages 24–26) can help you constrain conversations and attack difficult situations piece by piece. This helps you deal with only one small portion of negative energy at a time and keep your confidence.

- Authority voice—Using an authority voice (see page 26) is an essential self-protection skill. As explained earlier, you communicate authority by lowering the pitch of your voice at the end of a directive statement. It subconsciously tells the listener, "This is the way it is."

- Clarity in giving directives—When you present a directive, you want to keep the receiver focused and avoid setting the stage for confusion or debate. Remember the following strategies for telling difficult or resistant people what you expect them to do:

  - Think through what you are planning to say to the difficult or resistant staff member. Picture the details in your head, or put together a list of the ideas you want to address so you won't get lost in the emotions of the moment.

  - Be clear and direct when confronting the person. Try to use as few words as possible; don't worry about justifying your points. Just state the facts.

- Position/proximity—Sitting across from a difficult or resistant staff member at your desk conveys authority and power, both of which help control the energy in conversations. Standing up when confronting a difficult or resistant employee also helps convey power and minimizes your chances of being confronted or psychologically attacked.

- Room arrangement—This strategy is closely related to the position/ proximity strategy but has a few little variations. At times, difficult or resistant people try to manipulate situations in the conferencing room. You need to feel in control and in charge during the conference. Consider the following in setting up your office or meeting room when you meet with difficult or resistant staff members:

  - Raise your chair or lower the visitor's chair so you are sitting a little higher than the difficult or resistant staff member.

  - Consider sitting so that you block the exit or escape route. We have had staff members who got upset and reestablished control by running out of the office. They were so fast we couldn't catch them.

- Pacing of voice speed—If you focus on slower, more purposeful speech, it will convey seriousness on your part and allow you a chance to breathe while you are talking. Keeping your breathing deep and slow helps relax you and makes you less susceptible to attack.

- Reflecting statements—This strategy was introduced earlier in the book (see pages 23–24 and 86). Reflecting back the content and emotions of what the other person has said and combining his or her issues help keep you in control during your potentially confrontational conversations with difficult and resistant staff members.

Follow-Up

For any effort to be successful, an effective follow-up plan needs to be in place. In doing follow-up, you are trying to ensure that the efforts you have made, the skills you have taught, and the behaviors you have changed all become more permanent. Without follow-up, people will go back to their previous behaviors.

Let's see how one principal plans to follow up after a conference with a difficult staff member.

Scenario: The Negative Organizer

Maria, an elementary principal, is concerned about Angela, a staff member who has been causing problems at her school for several years. Angela resists all new ideas and changes and has begun to recruit others on the staff to join her in her opposition. Maria can see that Angela is starting to have a negative impact on the school climate.

Maria decides that she needs to address Angela's behavior and help her improve her attitude. Maria takes the time to think through specifically what Angela is doing to cause problems at the building. She uses this information to design a conference with Angela. At this conference, she clearly and confidently outlines her concerns about Angela's behavior and lays out her expectations for the steps Angela will take to eliminate her negative behaviors.

Maria tells Angela that she will help her stay on track with her improvement plan. She explains that she will meet with her on a monthly basis to talk about her progress toward eliminating her negative behaviors. In these follow-up meetings, Maria will give Angela feedback about her efforts to improve her behavior but will also give her the opportunity to share any concerns privately with Maria. Maria feels that these private conversations will allow Angela to vent without contaminating the rest of the staff. This process will help wean Angela off the habit of trying to engage other staff members in her negativity, as well as allow her to develop some kind of relationship with Maria. Over time, Angela's negative behavior will be replaced with positive problem-solving strategies.

Methods for Following Up With Staff Members

In the scenario just described, we saw how the strategic use of follow-up can help reshape a negative staff member's behavior. This is an important concept to remember and one that you will need to use as you begin to confront and reverse the impact of difficult or resistant people in your building.

Here are some follow-up methods that we have found helpful in working with difficult and resistant people and behaviors:

- Hold a conversation a week or so after confronting a behavior to make sure the person is still on track.

- Ask the person to report back to you a month after he or she has put into place the plan you helped develop.

- Stop by the classroom of a teacher you have worked with to eliminate a negative behavior, and ask that teacher to tell you about his or her progress in doing so.

- Meet with a team that previously had issues but is working on them through the implementation of group meeting norms.

- Send a note of encouragement to a staff member you previously worked with to change a negative behavior.

- Ask for a written report from a staff member whom you have helped to change a negative practice.

- Hold a follow-up meeting with the entire staff to talk about a concern that was brought up in an earlier planning meeting.

- Connect two staff members together in a mentoring relationship to help each other work through some issues; meet with them periodically to help them continue their progress.

- Offer optional problem-solving meetings in which people can share concerns and ideas about a new implementation.

- Set up periodic meetings with the difficult or resistant staff member to check progress and clarify behavioral expectations.

- Observe instruction in the difficult or resistant staff member's classroom, and make note of his or her progress in implementing the new practice or initiative.

- Break the difficult or resistant behavior into small parts. Work to improve the first part of the behavior, then move to a second part, third part, and so on. This type of plan can help ensure success.

- Establish behavioral benchmarks, and ask the staff member to report back as he or she reaches them.

Planning and Scheduling Follow-Up

The length of time necessary for follow-up to be effective varies. Even if you must deliver follow-up for an extended period of time, it is worth the effort to try to improve a staff member's behavior and attitude before taking more severe disciplinary steps. The exact amount of time required for the follow-up will depend on several factors. These factors include:

- The severity of the difficult or resistant behaviors

- The length of time the staff member has engaged in the difficult or resistant behaviors

- The length of time you have been the leader of the building

- Your perceived credibility as the leader

- The amount of reinforcement or support the difficult or resistant staff member is getting from others

- The extent to which the difficult staff member sees his or her behavior as a problem

- The extent to which the difficult or resistant staff member is invested in changing his or her behavior

- The quality and specificity of the follow-up plan

It is advisable to create a follow-up plan and schedule. The template provided in figure 9.1 can help you identify goals for the follow-up and a timeframe for reaching them.

Throughout the improvement process, you will need to constantly monitor and adjust your own efforts and the efforts of the difficult or resistant staff member you are working with. As is to be expected with any change initiative, the staff member will experience temporary setbacks and frustrating times. This is one reason you need to put together a comprehensive plan that will keep the person on track and moving forward.

Whole-School Follow-Up Strategies

We have talked about the importance of following up with individuals on your staff during a change effort, but it is equally important to follow up with and support the entire staff during a major change or implementation. Periodically looking at the change and how things are going is one key to a successful effort.

Identifying Issues and Opportunities

A good way to find out how things are going and to determine what needs to be addressed to keep the implementation moving forward successfully is to hold an open forum at a staff meeting. This conversation can be conducted in three stages:

1   Divide the large group into teams of four to six people. Give the teams about ten minutes to talk about what is working well with the implementation and what needs to be refined. To provide a structure for this conversation, distribute an outline or a worksheet similar to the one in figure 9.2 (page 106). Ask each small group to respond to the prompts and to be ready to share the results of its conversation with the entire group in stage 2.

2   The large group reconvenes, and each small group reports out the results of its conversation. As each group gives its report, one faculty member takes notes on chart paper. When every group has had a chance to report its findings, the group moves to stage 3 of the conversation.

Follow-Up Plan

Staff member:

Subject area:

Clear description of difficult or resistant behavior(s):

Clear description of new or desired behavior(s):

Behaviors that need to be reduced or eliminated in order to acquire the new or desired behavior(s):

Skills needed in order to learn or utilize the new or desired behavior(s):

Rank-ordering of behaviors to be reduced or eliminated:

Rank-ordering of skills or behaviors to be learned or acquired:

Schedule of behavior reduction:

Behavior	Month	Goal

Schedule of new skill or behavior acquisition:

Skill or Behavior	Month	Introduce (I) or Reinforce (R)

Figure 9.1: Template for planning follow-up.

Open Forum Conversation

It's important for us as a faculty to stop periodically and examine how our project is working. Please take a few minutes with your colleagues to discuss the following questions about the implementation of our project, and record your answers on this sheet. Once your small group has answered the questions, we will talk about the project as a whole group.

1. What steps of the project have been implemented to date? List any significant events related to the project or steps that we have accomplished.

2. What has gone well so far with the project? What progress have we made toward successful implementation? What positive impacts have you seen as a result of the implementation of the project?

3. What has not gone well so far with the project? What unresolved issues are still getting in the way of our success?

4. What strategies or suggestions do you have for us to overcome the challenges or limitations of this project and to be more successful in its implementation?

Figure 9.2: Worksheet for open forum conversation.

3   The entire faculty talks about the information that is listed on the chart paper. The group notes the trends it sees and proposes strategies to help minimize the concerns or negative impacts and maximize the positive developments. Then the group sets up a plan to use the strategies it has generated. Finally, the group creates a schedule for revisiting the implementation to continue to monitor its progress.

"How's It Going?" Activity

This activity has a similar purpose to the three-stage conversation just described, but it is conducted differently. At a faculty meeting, distribute a form like the one in figure 9.3 to every faculty member. Ask everyone to complete the form during the meeting and to return it to the school improvement team. The school improvement team reviews all of the submissions, tabulates the information, and reports it at the next faculty meeting. Then the team holds a conversation with the entire staff to help develop a plan to address the issues of greatest concern. The results of that planning are written up and distributed to the entire staff. The plan guides the work until the next implementation assessment is conducted, beginning once again with the distribution of the "How's It Going?" sheets. The length of time between assessments varies, depending on the depth of the project. We have found that some of the natural school-year divisions, such as quarters, semesters, and so on, are good times to repeat the administration of the "How's It Going?" feedback sheets.

How's It Going?

An important part of our success in this change effort is following up to make sure that we identify progress, problems, and concerns. We also need to work together as a faculty to find ways to support one another and address these concerns. Please take a few minutes to complete this assessment of our implementation. When you have completed it, please return it to a member of the school improvement team. We will tabulate the results and talk about them at our next faculty meeting.

List the aspects of the project that are moving along well or seem to be working well for you.	List the aspects of the project that are not going well or not working for you.	List possible ideas or strategies we need to consider to help overcome each issue or concern listed in the previous column.

Figure 9.3: "How's It Going?" feedback sheet.

Progress Reports

Another good way to find out how your project or change effort is going is to ask departments or grade levels to prepare short progress reports at regular intervals during the implementation (for example, on a quarterly basis). These reports can be fairly open ended, or you can provide an outline for their content so that you can keep everyone focused. Each school should determine what should be included in the progress reports to ensure that the most important information will be gathered and tabulated during the implementation. Here are some examples of content that will be helpful to you as you track your project:

- Updates on how much of the project has been successfully implemented

- Information about challenges or unanticipated problems that have arisen

- Specific examples of how teachers have implemented the project in their classrooms

- Details about positive impacts of the project implementation on students

- Quotes of unsolicited comments about or feedback on the project from students or parents

When you receive the progress reports, you can compile the information from them and share it with your staff either in written form or at a staff meeting.

Understanding the Unmet Needs of Your Staff

It is important for leaders to understand the needs that individuals and groups experience when they are asked to implement a change. The Concerns-Based Adoption Model identifies seven stages of concern that people go through during a new project or initiative (Hord, Rutherford, Huling-Auston, & Hall, 1987). Each stage of concern is associated with an unmet need. The researchers who developed the model contend that the unmet needs cause groups or individuals to become resistant to the new idea. They also point out that a person or group cannot move to higher levels of implementation until their needs at a particular level are met. Here are the stages of concern originally identified in the model:

1 Awareness

2 Informational

3 Personal

4 Management

5 Consequences

6 Collaboration

7 Refocusing

Table 9.2 (page 110) is a form we have developed to help us identify staff members' unmet needs at each stage of concern. Once we understand these needs, we can design interventions for the people who are already resistant to the change and take steps to prevent the others from becoming that way. Let's take a few minutes to walk through the first row of this chart.

At the awareness stage of concern, people simply need to know that something new is coming. If staff members are unaware of the coming change, this unmet need (column 2) will cause increased anxiety and aid in the development of difficult or resistant people in the building. In column 3, we have listed indicators that you may hear or see as a building leader that will give you a clue that awareness is the unmet need. Then in column 4, we offer strategies that can be implemented to fulfill the unmet need and minimize the anxiety at this concern stage.

We have found this information to be extremely helpful in managing change and transition and in helping understand and manage difficult or resistant people. If we determine that their difficulty or resistance is a product of an unmet need at one of the concern stages, it is easier to understand why they are negative, difficult, or resistant and to develop a plan to help them overcome these issues.

Looking at the unmet needs of group members is a good way to assess how a change process is going. It can also help you determine how to move forward while making sure to keep the project in a positive light.

Summary

In this chapter, you have learned about the importance of delivering effective follow-up to help difficult or resistant staff members stay on track with directed improvement efforts. As with any change process, the ongoing follow-up and support are crucial and sometimes more important than the initial plan. It is through the long-term support and follow-up that true change happens.

Follow-up may take extra time and attention, but it helps communicate to the employee that you care and want him or her to improve. This communication not only makes the employee feel supported but also sends a clear message that you will follow through on your expectations. The message has an impact beyond the person you are working to change; it lets everyone on the staff know and understand your priorities. Such clarity about your intentions will reduce the likelihood that other staff members at your school will become difficult or resistant.

Table 9.2: Stages of Concern and Unmet Needs

Concern Stage	Unmet Group Need	Indicators of Need	Strategies to Help Meet Group Needs
Awareness	The group is unaware that something new is coming.	Group members are unconcerned about the new program. People are moving forward with existing strategies or plans.	Use a visual technique to help the group become aware of the new idea or program. Present an overview of the new plan; have people meet in small groups to talk about it and develop a basic understanding.
Informational	The group needs specific information about the new idea and the degree of implementation that will be happening.	Group members openly complain that they don't know much about the new program. Group members criticize program leaders for the lack of information; they may exhibit "helpless" mentality.	Provide information in a visual manner, allowing interaction and dialogue between group members. Break implementation into parts; present parts and allow dialogue and group interaction.
Personal	The group or individuals in the group are not aware of how the new program will affect them.	Group members ask questions or complain about how the new idea affects them.	Set up activities to help group members personally connect with information.
Management	Group members have management concerns related to time, materials, coordination, and so on.	Group members ask questions or express concerns about the specifics of implementation.	Use group dialogue to come up with ideas about handling management issues.
Consequences	The group or individuals question whether students will benefit enough from the initiative to make it worth the effort.	Group members ask questions or express concerns about student benefits.	Structure dialogue at team meetings to find out people's experiences with students.
Collaboration	The group or individuals have concerns related to connections or working together.	Group members bring up questions about time to work together, merging philosophies, and so on.	Have group members share how they are working together; engage them in dialogue focused on problem solving.
Refocusing	The change or new program phase has been implemented; the group is interested in the next new implementation or phase to be added.	The group shows some comfort with the initial implementation and begins to ask questions about program variations or new implementations.	Engage the group in dialogue focused on implementation successes and challenges and the direction of the new project.

Questions for Reflection

Why is follow-up so important? How does it effectively contribute to the success of people trying to change their behaviors?

What skills can be helpful to you as you begin to confront the difficult and resistant people on your staff?

Why are planning and scheduling so important for a successful follow-up process? Why are regular interactions a part of the overall plan?

What have you learned in this chapter, and how do you think it will help you as you move forward in your efforts to work with difficult and resistant people?

chapter 10

Influencing Your Staff Members' Behaviors

As we all know, if we react to issues that have already developed, we may be less effective than if we had been able to prevent them in the first place. The preceding chapters have offered strategies for dealing with the eight types of difficult and resistant staff members once they have emerged and begun to present a challenge to you, the rest of the staff, and the school improvement initiative you are trying to implement. This concluding chapter will focus on ways to prevent difficult and resistant people from emerging in the first place and ways to minimize their impact if they do emerge.

As you read this chapter, you will learn the following:

- The importance of thorough planning
- Tips for staying alert and being proactive
- How to focus your energies for maximum effectiveness
- How to build a positive school climate and culture
- Ways to keep building your own skills and those of your staff members

The Importance of Thorough Planning

In previous chapters, we have pointed out ways that principals themselves might contribute to the development of particular difficult and resistant behaviors. What we want to stress here is that *ill-conceived plans related to program implementations* are often the root cause of negativity among staff members. A lack of forethought or a failure to have the necessary structures in place before launching school improvement initiatives gives staff members legitimate reasons to complain.

Thorough planning is crucial for staff buy-in. You must think through the details of your initiatives carefully. Be sure that you use a school improvement committee, planning council, or some other stakeholder group to help you determine your school's needs and the program or initiative that will best match these needs. As you and your group plan the initiative, it is particularly important to consider what the staff will need to start the implementation. For example, before a school improvement project begins, staff members need to have the necessary foundational information to understand precisely what they will be implementing and why. A lack of information naturally breeds difficulties and resistance.

Staying Alert and Being Proactive

As the school leader, you need to be on the lookout for signs that difficult and resistant people are emerging and gaining strength in your school. You also need to be aware of the kinds of situations in which they could potentially emerge. You want to guard against inadvertently contributing to the development of negativity within your staff—either by failing to recognize it or by failing to prevent it.

At the same time, you must realize that in any organization, it is important to have people who will raise reasonable questions about new ideas and initiatives. Without some form of disagreement, groups run the risk of developing "groupthink"—blindly pursuing an idea without considering possible dangers and problems. People who are skeptical about or question a plan do serve the purpose of getting a group to look at issues that might arise. The key word here is *reasonable*. As the leader, you should give staff members structured opportunities to talk about both the pros and cons of a new idea or initiative (chapters 1 and 3 suggest activities for facilitating such discussions). If, however, it seems that too many people are willing to take on an adversarial role or that some staff members are too strong in their skepticism or criticism, it is a signal that you should be monitoring the development of difficult and resistant people.

In the remainder of this section, we will point out several situations in which you might observe early warning signs of negative behavior. Being aware of these situations will help you to keep resisters from surfacing or from spreading their influence further.

The Interview Process

The interview process gives you the chance to look for negative tendencies in people before you actually hire them. Sometimes you can sense the issues that potential staff members might bring to your school. Notice candidates who seem to have an edge about them or who speak negatively about their present situation or leader. As a precaution, you may want to ask candidates to describe their present work situations or any issues they have experienced with their current supervisors. Being aware of and watchful for negativity in potential staff members may help you avoid taking on a new person who is difficult or resistant.

The Induction/Mentoring Process

When they first join the staff, some of our most promising new teachers can easily be influenced by others. Watch out for difficult or resistant staff members who may try to attach themselves to their new colleagues and influence them to join their ranks and also become difficult and resistant. Do your best to prevent this type of pairing up. Assign positive staff members to mentor your new teachers and help them build a solid foundation. Structure interactions with other positive people on the staff who aren't serving as formal mentors. Another way to minimize the impact of difficult and resistant staff members is to schedule new teachers' planning periods at different times from theirs.

Sudden Behavioral Changes

The fact that it is possible to define specific staff member types, as we have in the preceding chapters, suggests that most people are fairly predictable in their behaviors once they establish themselves on the staff. When you are aware of tendencies toward difficult and resistant behaviors, you can see them as they unfold. But you must also be alert to sudden changes in behaviors, which can signal that major problems are beginning to develop. Watch your staff carefully for behavior changes that may be clues that something is brewing. New relationships between staff members, staff members who become extremely isolated or staff members who develop extreme needs to be with other people, staff members who suddenly become quiet or staff members who suddenly become very vocal, staff members who are undergoing major life changes—all can be indicators of problems. If you notice such sudden behavior changes, study them and their impacts carefully for connections or patterns, and do what you can to head off any trouble you see developing.

Formation of Unlikely Alliances

This situation may seem related to the behavior changes just discussed but is more specific. When groups that were formerly at odds suddenly decide to work together, check into this development. It could be a sign that the group members are trying to increase their power and influence over the rest of the faculty. Think through the possible negative ramifications of this new alliance. Do the groups have a common agenda? Who will be involved in or influenced by the new alliance? Who is being left out of it? What impact might this have on the rest of the faculty members and their relationships? Thinking through these and other questions will help you as you work to minimize the development and influence of difficult and resistant staff members.

Focusing Your Energies for Maximum Effectiveness

It is important for you as the leader to determine the optimal use of your time and energies in dealing with difficult and resistant staff members. In this section, we will discuss several questions you should consider to guide your actions.

Is It Worth Your Time to Address the Behavior?

When difficult and resistant people start to throw rocks at your plan or innovation, your credibility is on the line. If you don't respond, the rest of your staff members may see you as weak and ineffective. In some isolated cases, however, you may actually be better off ignoring the behaviors of difficult and resistant staff members. Confronting these people may draw more attention to them and even help them gain staff sympathy.

Only you can decide the best course of action when negative behaviors surface in your own school, but here are some cases in which addressing the negative behaviors might cause more trouble than ignoring them:

- When the difficult or resistant staff member has no credibility with the rest of the staff
- When a majority of the staff is solidly behind the new initiative
- When the difficult staff member has developed sympathy from the rest of the staff members by leading them to believe that he or she has been picked on in the past
- When the staff member's negative remarks are legitimate and you have plans in place to rectify the problems
- When you are using your energy to support those who are implementing the new idea or change and your attention to the resister would steal their momentum

What Is Your Bottom Line?

What are your reasonable expectations for your staff members' conduct? What behaviors will you absolutely not tolerate? Many principals get into trouble and breed negativity when their bottom line is unclear or inconsistent. Difficult and resistant staff members thrive on ambiguity. By clearly identifying your bottom line and communicating your reasonable expectations to your staff, you minimize the chances that negative behaviors will emerge.

However, it's not enough just to communicate what you expect and then let nature take its course. You have to follow through with your attention and actions to let people know that you mean business. We have made this point several times, but we repeat it here because of its importance in minimizing the impact of negative people. Keeping this principle in mind will help you as you work to improve attitudes and move forward with your initiatives.

How Is Your Own Attitude Affecting Your Impact?

Your own attitude and behaviors have a lot to do with your success in preventing the emergence or flourishing of difficult and resistant staff members. Remember that you will achieve the best results if you can *stay positive* as you tackle the issues these staff members present. Of course, this is a challenging prospect. Here are some self-care strategies that you can use to keep from succumbing to the very negativity that you are trying to prevent in your school:

- Take care of your health; take the opportunity to exercise, and find additional ways to reduce stress.

- Engage with a colleague; find someone who will listen to you, offer ideas and strategies to help you deal with your situation, and keep what you share confidential.

- Put the situation you are dealing with in context. Acknowledge that it's important, but ask yourself, "Is this really a big deal?" Think through the behaviors you are seeing and ask yourself, "How does this situation compare to others that I may be dealing with in my life?" There is a good chance that you will decide that the problem is not as big of a deal as you first thought.

- Try to visualize the negative energy you are encountering, and shrink it in your head. Play through the scenarios you have been through, and gradually shrink them in your head.

- As you anticipate confronting difficult and resistant staff members, it is normal to think about the worst that could happen to you. Use the strategy of reframing, and think about the good that will come of the situation. Think about how well a meeting may go instead of focusing on what may go wrong. Also, visualize yourself winning in your confrontations with the difficult and resistant people on your staff. This will take some work, but if you visualize it, you can actually make it happen.

Building a Positive School Climate

A positive working climate goes a long way in helping to build the kinds of relationships and good will that keep difficult and resistant staff members from gaining strength or from surfacing in the first place. Treat your staff members with respect and professionalism, and let them know you expect the same from them. In most cases, people will live up to your expectations.

Staff meetings are an important tool for setting up a positive working climate. Work with your staff members to have them contribute to the success of your meetings. Many principals not only involve their staff members in planning the meetings but also ask them to present parts of the agenda. This strategy may help to decrease the incidence of negative and resistant behaviors because the ideas in the meeting come from colleagues rather than from the principal. In any event, plan your staff meetings so that everyone will be engaged and involved. Include activities for staff members to have fun and get to know more about one another. Short and engaging activities make difficult and resistant behaviors less likely.

Beyond staff meetings, look for other ways to make the working climate more engaging for your staff. Holding team events outside of the workday, allowing people a chance to get to know one another in different ways, showing an appropriate interest in employees' personal lives, and doing nice things for your staff members will always pay dividends in terms of a good working environment. If you believe that it is the principal's responsibility to get to know each person beyond his or her work skills, you will be making an important contribution to the overall school climate. As the leader, you set the tone. If you project a positive and engaging persona in your school, others will follow suit.

Building a Positive School Culture

School culture refers to the more enduring and stable foundation of behaviors, values, and attitudes that define a school. It is the summation of many interactions and events that work together to establish a track record of relationships. The culture of a school can either encourage or discourage the formation of difficult and resistant staff members. If your school has a culture in which it is acceptable for people to talk behind one another's backs, then it may be ripe for negativity. On the other hand, if an important part of your school culture is the development of norms that govern relationships and interactions, then difficult and resistant staff members are less likely to gain strength and power.

Even though the culture of a school is more established than the school's climate, which has more of a day-to-day nature, you can have an impact on it. Building a positive working climate over time will lead to a more positive culture. Helping your staff members create working norms will have a beneficial effect on the culture, as will helping them develop positive traditions and rituals. In the end, a strong, positive school culture will prevent negative and resistant behaviors from forming and gaining a foothold in your school.

Communication

Clearly, effective communication is one of the defining features of a positive school culture. In healthy and productive schools, principals spend time helping their staff members develop strong interpersonal skills. These skills will serve them well not only in their day-to-day operations with students and parents but also in their dealings with their colleagues, including those who are difficult and resistant. Staff meetings are an opportune time to address the development of communication skills.

Another way to ensure effective communication within a school is to provide staff members with formal vehicles or structures through which to express their concerns. For example, staff meetings can serve as open forums for bringing up and resolving issues. When staff members have questions or unresolved issues in relation to new initiatives, their anxiety levels rise. Times of high anxiety are perfect opportunities for difficult and resistant people to emerge and gain a foothold. You can lower the anxiety associated with new initiatives—and the chances for negativity to arise—by encouraging staff members to speak openly and providing prompt and clear responses.

We have found two structures to be particularly useful for giving staff members the chance to have their voices heard and their concerns addressed. These structures also give teachers new responsibilities and help them build leadership skills. The first is the building leadership team, and the second is the differentiated staff meeting.

The Building Leadership Team

The building leadership team (BLT) is a structure that effectively deals with school issues while developing and reinforcing teacher leadership. We have used BLTs in several buildings, and the strategy has virtually eliminated negativity and contributed to a more productive climate and culture. Here is a quick summary of how BLTs are set up and operated:

- Each grade level or content area has one representative on the BLT.

- The BLT meets monthly to discuss issues and provide input regarding the school improvement plan, data, intervention programs, and other issues.

- Each representative returns to the represented group to report on the issues discussed in the meeting.

The BLT provides teacher leadership opportunities and allows for a clear flow of information throughout the school. It is effective in defusing issues and proactively dealing with potentially negative behaviors.

The Differentiated Staff Meeting

As we have pointed out, staff meetings can be vehicles for a high level of communication. Unfortunately, because of time limitations and the size of faculties, they tend to be unproductive and used mostly for routine information sharing.

We have restructured staff meetings to maximize communication and problem solving, with great success. We refer to these reconfigured staff meetings as *differentiated* because they are designed to meet the diverse needs of staff members. At each meeting, staff members are divided into three groups:

1. Group A (Academics)—Staff members in this group discuss issues related to student learning and academics. Academic support staff members also attend this session to provide ideas and assistance to teachers who have student learning issues.

2. Group B (Behavior)—Staff members in this group discuss issues related to student behavior. Special education and behavior management team members attend this session to provide ideas and support.

3. Group C (Curriculum)—Staff members in this group discuss issues related to curriculum and standards. Instructional strategists and instructional coaches attend this session to provide ideas and support.

Each group is facilitated by a teacher leader, who uses an informational and processing form to guide discussions and keep the conversations positive and productive. Staff members leave the group meetings with practical ideas and strategies they have learned from their peers. This approach strengthens the school culture.

A typical staff meeting might look like this:

- Opening—Each meeting starts with a segment called Good News, in which staff members share news of positive developments. This helps shape the meeting and keep it more upbeat.

- General announcements—This section of the meeting, which usually takes only two or three minutes, is devoted to making timely announcements or sharing any personal information that is better delivered live than through email messages.

- Group meetings—Groups A, B, and C meet to discuss issues related to academics, student behavior, and curriculum.

- Summary and closing—Each group delivers a short report, and the meeting is adjourned.

The staff members rotate to a different group each meeting and so have an opportunity to participate in all of them during the course of a month.

The building leadership team and differentiated staff meetings help keep teachers in the loop, engaged, and therefore less susceptible to the influence of difficult and resistant staff members, should they surface.

A Culture of Fairness

One of the most important ways that you can build and maintain a positive school culture is to treat all your staff members fairly. A perception of either unfair treatment or favoritism creates negative feelings among staff members, which spread to affect the entire climate and culture of the school. These are the very foundations you are relying on to minimize the impact of difficult and resistant staff members. Make sure that you base your personnel decisions and dealings with individual staff members on sound principles, and then follow through to ensure a positive workplace for all.

Continuing to Build Skills

As you deal with difficult and resistant staff members, you may find yourself needing to expand your skill set with new ideas, techniques, and strategies. Consider continuing to build your skills by targeting your professional reading and attending workshops. Workshops not only help you acquire the necessary skills to deal with more complex behaviors but also let you meet and get to know others who have faced or are facing the same kinds of issues that you are facing. You will gain valuable colleagues whom you can trust for new ideas and support as you work with difficult and resistant staff members.

Just as developing your own skills is crucial for your success in dealing with difficult and resistant people, it is important that you find ways to help your staff members gain the information and skills they need to deal with their negative colleagues. You can recommend books and articles for staff reading groups, send key staff members to professional development sessions, or even conduct your own professional development sessions at your school. These sessions may be a part of a larger team-building effort or could be targeted to small groups or individuals. Some principals use their staff meeting time for skill-building and use other means of communication to disseminate routine information. Make sure your professional development sessions include an opportunity for staff members to practice the skills they are learning.

Summary

In this chapter, we have focused on the fact that principals can have considerable influence over their staff members' behaviors. It may be possible to prevent the emergence of difficult and resistant staff members entirely. It may be possible to diminish their impact if you notice that they are emerging. Or, if you lack the necessary awareness and alertness, it may be possible to actually encourage the development of these negative staff members through your policies and actions.

If difficult and resistant staff members are already operating in your school, it is important for you to assess your leadership approach to see how you might be contributing to the negative behaviors. But as you do so, keep in mind that difficult and resistant behaviors can be complex, and their causes can be difficult to pin down. If you understand your potential role in creating the behaviors, you may be able to diminish their strength while also making conditions more favorable for positive behaviors to take their place.

Once you have been able to break the cycle of negativity, you hold one of the keys to moving your school initiatives forward in a positive and productive manner. You will be able to focus your energies on addressing what your staff needs to carry out a successful implementation. Now it should be clear why negative staff members are so dangerous. They can hold the rest of the staff back from making the kinds of changes that will help our schools remain effective and that will allow us to have a positive impact on the lives of our students—the whole reason we are working so hard in the first place.

Questions for Reflection

How can you assess your leadership behaviors to see whether you are contributing to the problem of negativity at your school or to a productive work environment?

What strategies can you use to promote an effective school climate and ultimately improve the culture of the school?

What leadership behaviors might you be engaging in that could be reinforcing or strengthening difficult and resistant staff members?

Once you have identified the behaviors that have been contributing to the issues, how do you plan to minimize them?

What types of negative people seem to emerge in your school? What common complaints or issues seem to continually come up in staff members' conversations?

How does the day-to-day climate in your school impact the behaviors of difficult and resistant staff members? What factors in the school culture might contribute to the emergence of negative behaviors at your school?

References and Resources

Bramson, R. M. (1981). *Coping with difficult people.* New York: Dell.

Carnegie, D. (2009). *How to win friends and influence people.* New York: Simon & Schuster. (Original work published 1936)

Cloke, K., & Goldsmith, J. (2005). *Resolving conflicts at work: Eight strategies for everyone on the job.* San Francisco: Jossey-Bass.

Connors, N. (2000). *If you don't feed the teachers, they eat the students.* Nashville, TN: Incentive.

Dale Carnegie Training. (2009). *The five essential people skills: How to assert yourself, listen to others, and resolve conflicts.* New York: Simon & Schuster.

Eller, J. F. (2004). *Effective group facilitation in education: How to energize meetings and manage difficult groups.* Thousand Oaks, CA: Corwin Press.

Eller, J. F., & Eller, S. (2009). *Creative strategies to transform school culture.* Thousand Oaks, CA: Corwin Press.

Eller, J. F, & Eller, S. (2010). *Working with and evaluating difficult school employees.* Thousand Oaks, CA: Corwin Press.

Eller, S., & Eller, J. (2006). *Energizing staff meetings.* Thousand Oaks, CA: Corwin Press.

Fisher, R., & Uhry, W. (1991). *Getting to yes: Negotiating agreement without giving in* (2nd ed.). New York: Penguin.

Gill, L. (1999). *How to work with just about anyone: A three-step solution for getting people to change.* New York: Simon & Schuster.

Godwin, A. (2008). *How to solve your people problems.* Eugene, OR: Harvest House.

Goleman, D. (2006). *Emotional intelligence* (10th anniversary ed.). New York: Bantam.

Gorman, J. C. (2004). *Working with challenging parents of students with special needs.* Thousand Oaks, CA: Corwin Press.

Harvard Business School Press. (2005). *Dealing with difficult people.* Boston: Author.

Hord, S., Rutherford, W. L., Huling-Auston, L., & Hall, G. (1987). *Taking charge of change.* Alexandria, VA: Association for Supervision and Curriculum Development.

Jansen, J. (2006). *You want me to work with who? Eleven keys to a stress-free, satisfying, and successful work life—No matter who you work with.* New York: Penguin.

McEwan, E. (2005). *How to deal with teachers who are angry, troubled, exhausted, or just plain confused* (2nd ed.). Thousand Oaks, CA: Corwin Press.

Patterson, K., Grenny, J., Maxfield, D., McMillan, R., & Switzler, A. (2008). *Influencer: The power to change anything.* New York: McGraw-Hill.

Patterson, K., Grenny, J., McMillan, R., & Switzler, A. (2005). *Crucial confrontations: Tools for resolving broken promises, violated expectations, and bad behavior.* New York: McGraw-Hill.

Sanderson, V. (1999). *Life would be easy if it weren't for other people.* Thousand Oaks, CA: Corwin Press.

Stone, D., Patton, B., & Heen, S. (1999). *Difficult conversations: How to discuss what matters most.* New York: Penguin.

Sue, M. P. (2007). *Toxic people: Decontaminate difficult people at work without using weapons or duct tape.* Hoboken, NJ: Wiley.

Townsend, J. (2006). *Handling difficult people: What to do when people try to push your buttons.* Nashville, TN: Integrity.

Whitaker, T. (2002). *Dealing with difficult teachers* (2nd ed.). Larchmont, NY: Eye on Education.

bnl Index

Transforming School Culture: How to Overcome Staff Division
Anthony Muhammad
Busy administrators will appreciate this quick read packed with immediate, accessible strategies for transforming toxic school cultures into healthy environments conducive to change.
BKF281

Navigating Conflict and Feeling Good About It
Cassandra Erkens
This breakout session will help school leaders address conflict to elicit respect, improve rapport, and enable progress.
DVF037

Transforming School Culture: Understanding and Overcoming Resistance to Necessary Change
Anthony Muhammad
Dr. Muhammad addresses the major issues in the age-old battle of overcoming resistance to critical change. He provides tools to transform a school's culture into one that embraces the PLC model.
DVF022

Professional Learning Communities at Work: Best Practices for Enhancing Student Achievement
Richard DuFour, Robert Eaker
This classic resource offers practical information about transforming schools into learning-focused, results-oriented PLCs. Learn research-based recommendations for implementing PLC at Work® concepts.
BKF032

Leading With Trust: How to Build Strong School Teams
Susan Stephenson
Strategies, activities, and substantial findings from the latest research help teams identify causes of distrust, discuss taboo topics, and move toward a high-trust environment.
BKF282

a division of
Solution Tree | Press
Solution Tree

Visit solution-tree.com or call 800.733.6786 to order.

Wait! Your professional development journey doesn't have to end with the last pages of this book.

We realize improving student learning doesn't happen overnight. And your school or district shouldn't be left to puzzle out all the details of this process alone.

No matter where you are on the journey, we're committed to helping you get to the next stage.

Take advantage of everything from **custom workshops** to **keynote presentations** and **interactive web and video conferencing**. We can even help you develop an action plan tailored to fit your specific needs.

Let's get the conversation started.

Call 888.763.9045 today.